READ AHEAD

Reading and Life Skills Development

1

JO McENTIRE

Longman

Read Ahead 1: Reading and Life Skills Development

Pearson Education, 10 Bank Street, White Plains, NY 10606

Executive editor: Laura Le Dréan
Acquisitions editor: Lucille M. Kennedy
Development editor: John P. Barnes
Production editors: Diana P. George, Janice L. Baillie
Marketing manager: Joe Chapple
Senior manufacturing buyer: Edith Pullman
Photo research: Dana Klinek
Cover and text design: Ann France
Cover image: Jude Maceren/Stock Illustration Source, Inc.
Text composition: Rainbow Graphics
Text font: 11.5/13 Minion
Text art: Seitu Hayden/Wilkinson Studios, Inc.; Burmar Technical Corporation
Photo credits: **Page iii,** top to bottom: Neema Frederic/Corbis Sygma;
    Tom McCarthy/Photo Edit; © Jose Luis Pelaez, Inc./Corbis.
    Page 5, © Jose Luis Pelaez, Inc./Corbis. **Page 11,** © Michael
    Newman/Photo Edit. **Page 16,** © Comstock Images. **Page 33,**
    AP/Wide World Photos. **Page 34,** AP/Wide World Photos. **Page 38,**
    © Jasper James/Taxi/Getty Images. **Page 47,** top (left to right): © Eric
    Fowke/Photo Edit; © Park Street/Photo Edit; bottom (left to right): ©
    Robert Brenner/Photo Edit; © Steve/Mary Skjold/Index
    Stock Imagery. **Page 67,** © Steve Cole/Photodisc/Getty Images. **Page
    74,** Neema Frederic/Corbis Sygma. **Page 78,** © David Young-Wolff/Photo
    Edit. **Page 89,** AP/Wide World Photos. **Page 91,** AP/Wide World
    Photos. **Page 96,** © Jim Sugar/Corbis. **Page 112,** © ThinkStock
    LLC/Index Stock Imagery. **Page 119,** © Spencer Grant/Photo Edit.
    Page 130, © Bettmann/Corbis. **Page 164,** Tom McCarthy/Photo Edit.
    Page 188, © Jose Luis Pelaez, Inc./Corbis.

Library of Congress Cataloging-in-Publication Data

McEntire, Jo.
    Read ahead 1 : reading and life skills development / by Jo McEntire.
        p. cm.
    ISBN 0-13-118947-6
  1. English language--Textbooks for foreign speakers. 2. Reading
comprehension--Problems, exercises, etc. 3. Life skills--Problems,
exercises, etc. I. Title. II. Title: Read ahead one.

PE1128.M363 2005
428.6'4--dc22

                                                    2004020114

LONGMAN ON THE **WEB**

Longman.com offers online resources for
teachers and students. Access our Companion
Websites, our online catalog, and our local
offices around the world.

Visit us at **longman.com**.

Printed in the United States of America
1 2 3 4 5 6 7 8 9 10–VHG–08 07 06 05 04

Contents

Scope and Sequence iv
Introduction viii

CHAPTER 1
Getting Started 1

CHAPTER 2
From One Language to Another 24

CHAPTER 3
"Home Sweet Home" 47

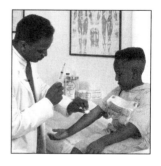

CHAPTER 4
Reaching Out Across the World 74

CHAPTER 5
The World of Work 101

CHAPTER 6
From One World to Another 130

CHAPTER 7
Health Matters 164

CHAPTER 8
Learning to Learn 188

Scope and Sequence

CHAPTER	READINGS	READING SKILLS	VOCABULARY SKILLS
1 Getting Started	Katya Valenski: A Pharmacist César González: A Computer Technician My Own Business	Previewing a reading	Previewing vocabulary Understanding phrasal verbs with *drop*
2 From One Language to Another	Writing of the Past Interpreting for the "Little Giant" Text Messaging: A New Language?	Previewing a reading Finding reasons Understanding pronouns	Previewing vocabulary Choosing the correct word form
3 "Home Sweet Home"	Living with a Host Family Finding an Apartment/ Moving In The Homeless in America	Previewing a reading Predicting	Previewing vocabulary Using context clues to understand vocabulary Understanding phrasal verbs with *get*
4 Reaching Out Across the World	Building a Home, Building a Life The Red Cross and the Red Crescent Earthquake! A Survivor's Tale	Previewing a reading Understanding general versus specific ideas Finding paragraph topics	Using context clues to understand vocabulary Previewing vocabulary Understanding phrasal verbs with *break*

LIFE SKILLS	WRITING ACTIVITIES	ONLINE ACTIVITIES
Introducing yourself and others	Sentence practice	Writing an e-mail to a friend
Understanding medicine labels	Paragraph practice	
Understanding e-mail		
Finding information on the Internet	Sentence practice	Using a search engine
	Paragraph practice	Locating a pharmacy
		Finding directions; printing maps
Reading numbers out loud	Sentence practice	Searching for apartments/host families
Understanding housing abbreviations	Paragraph practice	
Finding information on the Internet		
Completing more advanced Internet searches	Sentence practice	Finding your local Red Cross/Red Crescent
		Researching past events
		Narrowing an online search

CHAPTER	READINGS	READING SKILLS	VOCABULARY SKILLS
5 **The World of Work**	The Power of Networking Tips on Completing Applications How to Be Successful in an Interview	Previewing a reading Predicting	Using context clues to understand vocabulary Understanding present and past particle adjectives
6 **From One World to Another**	Culture Shock Caught Between Two Worlds Welcome to Gum Shan	Previewing a reading Finding the main idea of a paragraph Expanding previewing skills	Using context clues to understand vocabulary Previewing vocabulary Understanding the prefix *dis-*
7 **Health Matters**	The ABC's of Everyday Health How to Give CPR The Amazing Human Heart	Previewing a reading Scanning for information	Using context clues to understand vocabulary Previewing vocabulary Understanding phrasal verbs with *run*
8 **Learning to Learn**	How to Reduce Test Anxiety How Does Memory Work? Pineapple St. Paul	Previewing a reading Understanding main ideas Reading between the lines	Using context clues to understand vocabulary Previewing vocabulary Choosing the correct word form

LIFE SKILLS	WRITING ACTIVITIES	ONLINE ACTIVITIES
Understanding the importance of networking

Completing applications

Being successful in an interview | Answering interview questions

Writing a dialogue

Completing a job application | Completing an advanced search

Researching do's and don'ts of interviewing

Finding sample interview questions |
| Asking for and giving advice

Making compromises | Paragraph practice: explaining a problem

Writing from notes

Writing a letter | Completing an advanced search

Finding out about reverse culture shock

Researching the past: The Gold Rush and Lalu Nathoy |
| Explaining how to do something

Finding basic medical information online | Paragraph practice: describing a process

Labeling a diagram | Using quotation marks to narrow the search field

Finding medical information online

Locating the nearest CPR classes |
| Setting realistic goals | Completing a chart

Writing a dialogue

Describing goals

Finishing a short story | Locating tips to answer multiple-choice questions

Researching examples of mnemonic cues

Finding practice GED questions |

Introduction

Teachers today are faced with the challenge of meeting more diverse student goals than in the past. While life and workplace skills are critical to the success of students, employment trends indicate that students also need higher-level academic skills to succeed and advance in the workplace. *Read Ahead 1* recognizes the need for teachers to blend this variety of skills by helping students develop skills to read with confidence, make informed decisions, work cooperatively, and understand how they learn.

Text Organization

Read Ahead 1 has eight chapters, each consisting of three thematically linked readings. The opening page of each chapter includes a brief description of the readings and a preview of the reading, vocabulary, and life skills practiced in the chapter. Chapters are organized as follows:

Before You Read

Before each reading, students are asked questions to activate their knowledge about the subject of the reading. Key vocabulary is previewed to aid students' comprehension of the reading and to encourage fluency.

Now Read

Each of the three chapter readings explores a different aspect of one theme. Throughout the book, students read a variety of text types, ranging from exposition to interviews and short stories.

After You Read

Each reading is followed by *How Well Did You Read?* and *Check Your Understanding* questions. These exercises focus on students' general understanding of the reading. Additional exercises focus on specific skills introduced in the chapter, allowing students to practice and apply these skills.

Expanding the Topic

Located at the close of each chapter, this section includes writing topics that encourage students to use the vocabulary and content they have learned *(Connecting Reading with Writing),* and asks students to find out more about the topics by completing guided online searches *(Exploring Online).*

Reading, Vocabulary, and Life Skills

Reading, vocabulary, and life skills are clearly and concisely presented in skill boxes throughout each chapter and are recycled throughout the book. Reading skills include previewing, predicting, identifying topics and main ideas in a paragraph, and inferring information. Vocabulary skills include guessing meaning through context, understanding word forms and understanding phrasal verbs. Life skills address topics such as sending e-mail, making introductions, understanding medicine labels, reading advertisements, completing applications, and setting goals.

Vocabulary Review

Each chapter concludes with a review of vocabulary introduced and targeted within that chapter. This is a quick and effective way for both teachers and students to assess their understanding of this vocabulary. The first exercise is a cloze activity, and the second requires students to use the vocabulary in their own words.

As students progress through this text, they will work with classmates to develop confidence in reading and talking about reading. Because of the carefully chosen themes, students will understand that they already know a great deal, and that this prior knowledge facilitates more learning. They will become more independent learners as they approach the transition to academic studies.

Teacher's Manual

The teacher's manual includes general 'teaching the chapter' guidelines, teaching suggestions for specific chapters, and Chapter Review Tests. Each test includes vocabulary items from the chapter and comprehension questions about a reading passage related to the chapter theme. The tests are designed to be given within a class period, and provide valuable feedback to students and teachers about student progress in building reading and vocabulary skills. Answer keys for the student book exercises and Chapter Review Tests are also provided.

About the Author

Jo McEntire has been an English language instructor for over twenty years. She is on the faculty of Shoreline Community College in Seattle, Washington, where she has served as Director of Adult Basic Education as well as Program Chair for English language learning. Ms. McEntire has also taught in Botswana, Africa, and Oman. She is a graduate of Manchester University in England.

Acknowledgements

I would like to thank Laura Le Dréan and Lucille M. Kennedy for their continuing support, John P. Barnes for his thoughtful and constructive editing, Diana P. George and Janice L. Baillie for their fine production work, and Dana Klinek for her excellent photo research. Thanks also to the reviewers whose comments on early drafts of this book were very helpful: Marsha Abramovich, Tidewater Community College, Virginia Beach, VA; Susan Jamieson, Bellevue Community College, Bellevue, WA; Paula Sanchez, Miami-Dade College, Miami, FL; Alice Savage, North Harris Community College, Houston, TX. In addition, I wish to thank the faculty at Shoreline Community College for the sabbatical that allowed this text to be written. Finally, thanks again to my family for making sure that writing never gets in the way of horses, soccer, and the evening meal. Balance is everything.

Jo McEntire

Getting Started

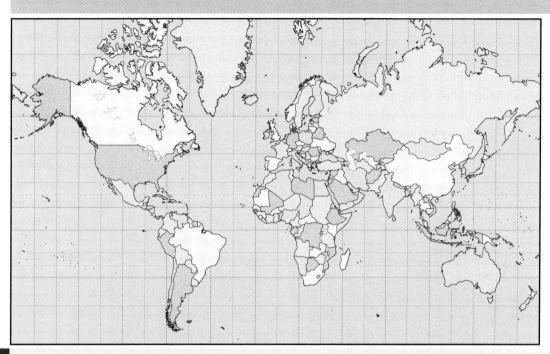

This chapter is about starting to work in the United States. In Reading 1, you will meet a woman from Ukraine who became a pharmacist. Reading 2 introduces you to a man who went to college to take some computer classes and then began working there. The last reading is an interview with a man who has his own business.

In this chapter, you will practice:

Reading Skills
→ Previewing a reading

Vocabulary Skills
→ Previewing vocabulary
→ Understanding phrasal verbs with *drop*

Life Skills
→ Introducing yourself and others
→ Understanding medicine labels
→ Understanding e-mail

Before You Read

Knowing how to introduce yourself is an important skill. It is the first step in getting to know your classmates and your co-workers. You will enjoy class and work more if you meet the people there and make friends. When you enjoy English class and your workplace, you will learn more English!

Life Skill

Introducing Yourself and Others

You can introduce yourself at school this way:

"Hi. My name is Maria. It's nice to meet you."

"It's nice to meet you, too. I'm Natalya. Is this your first English class, Maria?"

You can introduce yourself at work this way:

"Good morning. My name is Lee. I'm looking forward to working with you."

You can introduce a friend this way:

"Hi, Peter. I'd like you to meet a friend of mine, James. James, this is Peter."

"Hi, Peter. Nice to meet you."

"Hi, James. Nice to meet you, too. Do you live near school, James?"

How do you address a person you don't know very well?

In America, it is often difficult to figure out if we should call people by their first name, or by their last name with a title (Mr. Chang, Mrs. Peters).

- Students usually call each other by their first name: Lee, Vladimir, Juan.
- At work, you should use Mr., Ms., or Mrs. to address your boss. Your boss will say, "Call me José," if he wants to be informal.

If you are not sure, it is always okay to ask, "What should I call you?"

Work in small groups. Introduce yourself to your group. When you have all introduced yourselves, practice introducing each other. Use the introductions on page 2 to help you.

1. Ask your teacher what he or she wants to be called. Introduce your group to your teacher.

2. Turn to page 1 and look at the world map. Think about other countries or cities where you have lived or visited. Introduce yourself to the group again. Tell them where you are from or talk about some places you have visited. Say, "Hi. My name is *Roberto*. I'm from *Puerto Rico*. Where are you from?"

Reading Skill

Previewing

A good soccer player always warms up before running onto the field to play a game. In the same way, a good reader previews before reading something new. **Previewing** prepares you to read.

To preview,

- read the title and look at the illustrations. This will give you a general idea of the reading.
- think about what you already know about the subject. Have you read any books about it? Have you learned about it in school? Do you have any experience with it?

After you preview, you are ready to read.

The questions at the beginning of each reading will help you preview. Be sure to answer these previewing questions before you begin the reading.

Previewing

Discuss the questions with a partner.

1. Look at the title of Reading 1. Look at the photo on page 5. What is this woman's job?

2. How do people get this job? Is it a good job? Why or why not?

Previewing Vocabulary

These words are in Reading 1. Read the words and their definitions. Then choose the best word or words to complete each sentence.

Word	Definition
passed away	died
single parent	a mother or father who is raising a child alone
transfer	move something or someone from one place to another
urgent	very important
prescription	medicine that a doctor orders for a patient
dosage	a measured amount of medicine
side effects	effects of a drug that are not intended
allergic	not able to touch or eat something because it makes you sick
health insurance	a company policy that helps pay medical costs if you get sick or have an accident
accurately	carefully, without making mistakes

1. My son had a bad earache, so the doctor wrote a _____ for some medicine.

2. I am _____ to cats. If I touch them, my eyes begin to hurt, and I start to sneeze.

3. Some medicines have serious _____. For example, some allergy medicines make you very sleepy.

4. Doctors fill out prescription forms very _____. They don't want to make a mistake and write down the wrong medicine.

5. "What's the daily _____ for these drugs?"
   "You take one tablet three times a day."

6. "You have an _____ call from your husband. He says you must call him at once."

7. Being a _____ is not easy. It is very hard sometimes for one parent to look after children.

8. When I finish my English class, I want to _____ to a university to study business.

9. We were very sad when our grandfather _____. He was ninety-nine years old when he died.

10. My company gives me _____, so I don't need to pay the doctor when I get sick.

Now Read

Katya Valenski: A Pharmacist

1   My name is Katya Valenski, and I am from Kiev, Ukraine. My husband passed away when we lived in Kiev. Our daughter was only two at that time. Life was very difficult. It is never easy to be a single parent. Then my friend entered me in the Green Card lottery[1] without telling me. I won! When she first told me this, I didn't believe her. I didn't know what to do. I didn't know if I wanted to live in another country. My sister was living in Texas. I thought about it for a long time. Then I decided my daughter and I would join her.

2   Life was not very easy during the first few years in America, but I was lucky to have my sister and her family to help me. I had to learn how to drive and get a job. I had to go to community college to learn more English. It took a long time. My daughter was just three when we arrived, but she started to speak English very quickly. Soon, her English was better than my English.

3   As my English improved, I began to think carefully about my future. As a single mother, I needed a job that paid well. I decided to become a pharmacist.[2] I finished English lessons and began to take college courses. My adviser at the college helped me transfer some of my school courses from Kiev University. I didn't have to take these courses again in Texas. I got my two-year associate's degree in science, and then I transferred to a four-year school. It took a long time to finish my degree in pharmacy. Luckily, I got financial aid to help pay for the classes. I also continued to work while I was in school.

4   I am now a pharmacist. I love my job. When I arrive at work, I check my voice mail. I always have messages from patients and doctors or nurses. I listen to every message. I take notes while I am listening. If there is an urgent message, I call back immediately. Most of the messages are for new prescriptions. In this pharmacy, people can call in or e-mail their prescriptions. Then I log on to my computer. I

---

[1] **Green Card lottery:** a chance to win a Green Card

[2] **pharmacist:** a person who prepares the medicine ordered by a doctor

continued

check my e-mail. More messages! Every day begins like this. When I finish checking my e-mail, I make up the new prescriptions. I must be very careful. Each time I make a prescription, I put the information in the computer.

5   I enjoy helping people. When patients come to pick up their prescriptions, I always make sure they understand the doctor's instructions. I make sure they know the dosage. It is very important to take the correct amount of medicine. Patients can become seriously ill if they take too much medicine. Patients should also know about side effects. Some medicines, for example, make you sleepy. Other medicines give you a stomachache unless you take them with food. Finally, I check to make sure that the person is not allergic to the medicine. If you are allergic to a medicine, you must not take it because it can be dangerous.

6   Another important part of my job is completing health insurance forms. About half of my patients have health insurance. There are many different kinds of insurance. Each insurance plan is different. The forms are complicated and difficult to complete accurately. If I make a mistake, the patient sometimes has to pay too much money, so I must be careful.

7   All day people come and ask me questions about different medicines. They ask me questions about prescription drugs and over-the-counter drugs. Over-the-counter drugs are medicines you can buy without a prescription from your doctor. I help people choose the best over-the-counter medicine for their illness.

8   This is a 24-hour pharmacy, so at 6:00 p.m. the evening pharmacist begins work. On the way home, I pick up Anna from her after-school daycare. We cook dinner together and talk about our day. Later, while Anna does her homework, I wash the dishes. Then we watch TV together. By 9:30, we are both in bed.

After You Read

How Well Did You Read?

Work with a partner. Read the statements. Write *T* (true) or *F* (false).

_____ 1. Katya, her husband, and her daughter moved to Texas to live with her sister.

_____ 2. Life was not easy for Katya when she first arrived in Texas.

_____ 3. Katya wanted a good job to support her child.

_____ 4. Katya didn't need a degree to be a pharmacist.

Check Your Understanding

Circle the letter of the best answer.

1. Katya moved to Texas _____.

   a. one year before her husband died
   b. one year after her husband died
   c. several years after her husband passed away

2. When Katya won a Green Card _____.

   a. she was very happy because she wanted to come to America
   b. she was very surprised because she didn't know she was in the lottery
   c. she immediately got on a plane and flew to Texas

3. The first few months in America were not easy because _____.

   a. Anna learned English quickly
   b. Katya's sister helped her learn about America
   c. Katya couldn't drive and didn't know much English

4. Katya did not have to take some courses in Texas because _____.

   a. she didn't have enough money
   b. she didn't enjoy these courses
   c. she had already taken these courses in Kiev

5. As soon as Katya arrives at work each day, _____.

   a. she drops off her daughter at school
   b. she listens to her telephone messages and then logs on to her computer
   c. she checks her e-mail and prepares the new prescriptions

6. Prescription drugs can be dangerous if _____.

   a. the patient is very ill
   b. the patient is allergic to the drugs
   c. the patient takes the correct amount of medicine

7. Katya tells the patients _____.

   a. which over-the-counter medicines are best for them
   b. which prescription drugs are best for them
   c. which health insurance is best for them

8. After work, Katya _____.

   a. drives home, makes dinner, and then picks up her daughter from daycare
   b. picks up her daughter from daycare, and then drives home
   c. drives straight home and meets her daughter there

Understanding Medicine Labels

It is important to understand the information on a label for prescription medicine. Every year, many people get sick or have accidents because they do not or cannot read prescription labels accurately. If you don't understand the label, you should always ask the pharmacist to help you.

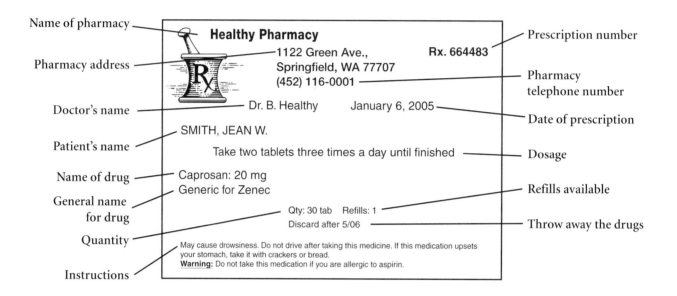

Name of pharmacy

Pharmacy address

Doctor's name

Patient's name

Name of drug

General name for drug

Quantity

Instructions

Healthy Pharmacy
1122 Green Ave.,
Springfield, WA 77707
(452) 116-0001

Rx. 664483

Dr. B. Healthy   January 6, 2005

SMITH, JEAN W.

Take two tablets three times a day until finished

Caprosan: 20 mg
Generic for Zenec

Qty: 30 tab   Refills: 1
Discard after 5/06

May cause drowsiness. Do not drive after taking this medicine. If this medication upsets your stomach, take it with crackers or bread.
Warning: Do not take this medication if you are allergic to aspirin.

Prescription number

Pharmacy telephone number

Date of prescription

Dosage

Refills available

Throw away the drugs

A. Read the prescription medicine label. Work with a partner to ask and answer the questions. Use the information from the label. One of you is the pharmacist and the other is the customer. Then change roles and repeat the exercise.

1. What is the name of the medicine?

2. How much should I take, and how often should I take it?

3. How long do I need to take this medicine?

4. Are there any side effects?

5. I am allergic to aspirin. Can I still take this medicine?

B. Use the information from the prescription drug label to complete the following paragraph.

On May 4, ___Jean Smith___ went to see her doctor because she felt sick. She had a fever and a sore throat. Her doctor, _____, did some tests and found that Ms. Smith had an infection. He wrote her a prescription for _____. This drug is the same as _____, but it is less expensive. The doctor told Ms. Smith to take _____ tablets _____ a day. She had to take the tablets for _____ days. He warned her not to _____ because the drug could make her sleepy. He told her to take the medicine with _____ because it sometimes _____ people's stomachs. If Ms. Smith continued to have a sore throat after she finished all the tablets, she could return to the pharmacy for a _____. She must give the _____ number to the pharmacist to get more medicine. Finally, the doctor asked Ms. Smith if she was _____ to aspirin.

Reading 2 *César González: A Computer Technician*

Before You Read

Previewing

Discuss the questions with a partner.

1. Read the title and look at the photo on page 11. What kind of job does this person have?

2. Do you think this is a good job? Would you like this job? Why or why not?

3. Do you think this person had to go to college before he got this job? Why or why not?

Previewing Vocabulary

These words are in Reading 2. Read the words and their definitions. Then choose the best word or words to complete each sentence.

Word	Definition
majored in	studied as a main subject in college
tuition	the money you pay for classes
install software	put new computer programs on a computer
trouble-shooting	finding and fixing problems
password	a secret word that you use to open your computer
delete	remove some information from a computer
freezes	stops working
frustrated	feeling a little angry
computer virus	a secret program that someone puts into a computer to destroy computer files
posts	puts information on a Web site

1. I opened an e-mail that said, "I love you." However, it was a _____. It destroyed all my computer files.

2. My teacher _____ our tests on her Web site so that we can take tests at home.

3. Young-hee _____ pharmacy when she was in college. She is now a pharmacist.

4. It is easy to _____ on a computer. You just follow the instructions on the new software.

5. At work, I have to use a _____ to log on to my computer. I wrote this word on the back of my dictionary so I won't forget it.

6. When my computer _____, I turn it off for a few minutes. When I turn it back on, it works again.

7. _____ for a four-year university is more expensive than for a community college. Many students begin their education at a community college to save money.

8. Tom is very good at _____ car problems. He can always find the problem and fix it.

9. I often get _____ learning English. English is a difficult language to learn. I spend a lot of time learning words, and then I forget them.

10. I get a lot of e-mail from people I don't know. I always _____ these messages because I don't want to read them.

Now Read

César González: A Computer Technician

1   César González lives in San Diego, California. His parents moved from Mexico to the United States when he was ten years old. César couldn't speak any English when he first arrived, but he soon began to learn the language. He learned English more quickly than his parents. He often helped his mother and father when they didn't understand some words. When he graduated from high school, César could speak both English and Spanish very well.

2   César loves computers. When he was a child, he loved playing computer games. In high school, he took several computer classes. When he finished high school, he decided he wanted to work with computers. He went to the local community college and majored in computer technology. César was an excellent student, and his instructor often asked him to help other students. If a computer broke down, the instructor asked César to fix it. César was so good at fixing computers that the instructor offered him a job. César was very happy because he loved working with computers, and he needed the money to pay his tuition. When he graduated a year later, the college offered him a full-time job.

3   César is a morning person. He loves getting up very early. This is lucky because he has to start work at seven every morning. He leaves home at six-thirty because even this early, the traffic is very bad. César's job is to help the faculty with any computer problems. He also has to install new software and teach the instructors to use this software. He is very busy because there are more than two hundred instructors and only two technical support advisers. He likes being busy, however, because the time passes very quickly. He never gets bored at work.

continued

4 As soon as César arrives at work, he puts on the coffee. While the coffee is brewing, he checks his voice mail and his e-mail. He spends every morning trouble-shooting faculty computers. He usually has lots of messages from faculty asking for help. Some teachers forget their password and cannot log on to their computers. Some teachers delete files by mistake. Sometimes, a teacher's computer freezes, and the teacher doesn't know what to do. These are very simple problems. César sometimes gets frustrated with the faculty. He thinks they should be able to fix these problems themselves.

5 However, sometimes the problems are serious. If a computer breaks down, César must fix it without losing the teacher's files. Computer viruses are another serious problem. Sometimes a virus is e-mailed to the college. If someone opens this e-mail, the virus can destroy computer files. It can also spread very easily through e-mail to other college computers.

6 César has lunch at eleven-thirty, and then he works out in the college gym for thirty minutes. In the afternoon, he teaches computer classes to the faculty. He teaches them how to set up their own Web site. The faculty can then use their Web site to post information about their classes. They can post their homework and tests on the Web site.

7 César shares an apartment with a friend. After work, he usually has a quiet evening. The weekends, however, are a different story! César loves to party, and he has lots of friends. He loves Latin music,[1] and he and his friends often go out to clubs where Latin bands are playing. He also likes camping. César believes you should work hard and play hard, and he does both!

[1] **Latin music:** music coming from Mexico or South or Central America

After You Read

How Well Did You Read?

Read the statements. Write *T* (true) or *F* (false).

_____ 1. César has always enjoyed using computers.

_____ 2. César got his first job when he graduated with his degree.

_____ 3. César likes most of his work.

_____ 4. César enjoys quiet weekends.

Check Your Understanding

Circle the letter of the best answer.

1. César became interested in computers _____.

    a. when he started high school
    b. after he finished high school
    c. before he started high school

2. César began to work for the college _____.

    a. while he was still a student
    b. after he graduated
    c. before he took computer courses

3. His teacher asked him to work because _____.

    a. César needed money to pay for his tuition
    b. César was a very good student
    c. he knew César wanted a job

4. César sometimes gets frustrated at work because _____.

    a. he thinks instructors should know more about their computers
    b. he must wake up very early to get to work on time
    c. his job gets very busy every day at lunchtime

5. César thinks that deleting a file by mistake is _____.

    a. a difficult problem
    b. not a difficult problem
    c. something instructors like to do

6. A virus is a serious problem because _____.

    a. it destroys computer files
    b. it cannot move easily to other computers
    c. you need it to open an e-mail

7. A teacher's Web site _____.

    a. helps students because they can find a lot of information about the class
    b. helps the students because they can telephone the teacher for information
    c. gives all the answers so students don't need to study

8. César enjoys _____.

    a. going to clubs during the week
    b. fixing simple problems for the faculty
    c. listening to music during the weekend

Vocabulary Skill

Understanding Phrasal Verbs with Drop

Sometimes the verb in a sentence is really two or three words used together. This is called a **phrasal verb.** Each word is usually easy to understand. When the words are together, however, they have a different meaning. For example, here are some phrasal verbs with the word *drop.* Notice that the meaning of each phrasal verb is very different.

Examples:

drop in	visit someone without calling first
drop off	take someone to a place in a car
drop out	leave school or college before you finish your studies

A. Work with a partner. These phrasal verbs are in Reading 2. Find and underline the words in the reading. Then match the phrasal verb with the correct definition.

_____ 1. work out   **a.** start something

_____ 2. major in   **b.** use a password to start the computer

_____ 3. set up   **c.** choose a main subject at college

_____ 4. log on   **d.** stop working

_____ 5. break down   **e.** exercise

B. Choose the best phrasal verb to complete each sentence. Use the simple past tense.

1. Last night, I _____ at the gym for two hours.

2. Van's car _____ on the freeway. He called his friend to come and help him fix the car.

3. I like helping people, and I am interested in science. When I was at college, I _____ medicine because I wanted to be a doctor.

4. My friend _____ his own Web site full of information about fixing computers. It has very helpful information.

5. I _____ to my computer and found I had several new messages.

14   Read Ahead 1

Before You Read

Previewing

Discuss the questions with a partner.

1. Look at the photo on page 16. What job does this person have?

2. This reading is about having your own business. What are some good things about having your own business? What are some bad things about having your own business?

Previewing Vocabulary

These words are in Reading 3. Read the words and their definitions. Then choose the best word or words to complete each sentence.

Word	Definition
entrepreneur	someone who starts his or her own business
landscaping business	a company that designs and looks after gardens and parks
mows lawns	cuts grass in gardens, yards, or parks
borrowed	used something that belongs to someone else and gave it back later
expand	become bigger
clients	customers, people who pay for service from a business
accounts	written records of money

1. My teenage daughter _____ as a summer job. She charges ten dollars to cut your grass.

2. John W. Nordstrom was a successful _____. He began by selling shoes from a cart in the 1890s. Today his clothing stores are all over the United States.

3. It's important to keep your _____ accurate. You need to know how much money you have.

4. When my business began to _____, I bought a bigger store. The business continued to grow.

5. When we moved into our new house, the yard looked terrible. The grass was dead, and it was very ugly. We called a _____ to help us improve the yard.

continued

6. Always be polite to your _____. They are the most important part of your business.

7. When Jim went to college, he _____ money from his uncle. He needed this money to pay for the college tuition.

Now Read

My Own Business

1 Nick Petrovic is one of Littleton's most successful entrepreneurs. He owns the largest landscaping business in the city. Earlier today, he took time out of his busy schedule to sit down with me and talk about his success story.

2 **Reporter:** Nick, why did you decide to start your own business? Why didn't you find a job like most people do?

3 **Nick:** Well Pat, I never really decided to work for myself. It just happened. When I was a kid, I was very good at doing small jobs around the neighborhood. I mowed lawns and looked after younger kids. I was good at saving money. When I was a teenager, I used my savings to buy my own lawnmower. By the time I was sixteen, I was mowing about twenty lawns a week. I earned good money, and I enjoyed it.

4 **Reporter:** So how did you build your business from one lawn mower to the huge company you have today?

5 **Nick:** Good luck and hard work! When I was nineteen, I borrowed money from my parents to expand the business. I hired a friend to help me. I taught him to be very polite to clients. In business, the client is always right. You have to make the client feel special. Then they give you more

business. They also tell their friends about you, so you get new clients. Your business keeps growing, and suddenly you are successful.

6 **Reporter:** What about all the paperwork? The accounts and taxes and insurance? How did you learn to keep accurate accounts?

7 **Nick:** Good question. That is one part of the business I don't like very much. But, in a business, you must

continued

---

keep very accurate accounts. You must know how much money is coming in, and how much money is going out. At first I kept a notebook. I wrote everything down in that notebook, but the business became too busy. I realized I had to computerize my paperwork. Another friend helped me set up a program for accounts on the computer. This program is easy to use. I also took some college classes. I learned a lot about computers and business. Now I can't live without my computer and my e-mail.

8 **Reporter:** So how many people do you employ today?

9 **Nick:** Spring through fall is our busiest time. I have about 40 employees during this time. In the winter, I go down to about 25.

10 **Reporter:** What's the best thing about being your own boss?

11 **Nick:** It's exciting! Every day is different. I meet lots of people, and I have to make a lot of decisions. I'm not the kind of guy who can sit at a desk all day! I love going to different places and talking with people.

12 **Reporter:** What qualities does a person need to be a good entrepreneur?

13 **Nick:** You must be strong, and you must believe in yourself. You need good ideas, and you must be organized. You have to enjoy working hard. In fact, after a fourteen-hour day, I sometimes think you need to be a little crazy to have your own business!

14 **Reporter:** What's the worst thing about being your own boss?

15 **Nick:** If I make a mistake, I lose money. If I don't work hard, I'll lose the business. I sometimes worry something will go wrong with my business. I have a family to support. But, knock on wood,[1] everything is going well so far. Now, excuse me, Pat, I've got to run. I'm meeting with a client, and I don't want to be late.

16 **Reporter:** Thanks for your time, Nick. Good luck with your business.

[1] **Knock on wood:** an expression people use when they hope good luck will not become bad luck

After You Read

How Well Did You Read?

Read the statements. Write *T* (true) or *F* (false).

_____ **1.** Nick has always been a good businessman.

_____ **2.** Nick took some college classes to become a better businessman.

_____ **3.** Nick thinks money is more important than clients.

_____ **4.** Nick has a lot of time to talk with the reporter.

Check Your Comprehension

Circle the letter of the best answer.

1. How do you know Nick is a successful entrepreneur?

    a. He now owns a big, successful business.
    b. He mowed lawns when he was a child.
    c. He went to college.

2. When Nick was sixteen, _____.

    a. he began to mow lawns
    b. he hired a friend to help him with his business
    c. he mowed around twenty lawns every week

3. When Nick first wanted to expand his business, he _____.

    a. asked his parents for advice
    b. hired forty employees
    c. borrowed money from his parents

4. Nick believes the secret to a successful business is _____.

    a. to borrow money
    b. to ask for help from friends
    c. to be very good to your clients

5. Nick decided to put his accounts on the computer when _____.

    a. a friend told him to do this
    b. he became too busy to use a notebook for paperwork
    c. he went to college and learned about computers

6. During the winter, Nick's business _____.

    a. is busier than in the summer
    b. is less busy than in the summer
    c. closes down because it is cold

7. Nick is a person who _____.

    a. likes going to an office every day
    b. enjoys doing different things every day
    c. loves doing his accounts

8. Nick sometimes worries that _____.

    a. he is too busy and can't spend enough time with his family
    b. he will lose his business, and he won't have money for his family
    c. he has to make too many difficult decisions

9. Nick thinks that an entrepreneur needs to be a little crazy because
   _____.

   a. entrepreneurs do not always earn money
   b. a business is not always successful
   c. you have to work long, hard days

10. Nick has to leave the reporter because _____.

   a. he is late for a meeting with a client
   b. he doesn't want to be late for a meeting with a client
   c. he has to go running

Life Skill

Understanding E-Mail

E-mail is short for **electronic mail,** or messages you send through the Internet. Today, almost every business and millions of people all over the world have e-mail. Many of them use e-mail for most of their communication.

English has many words to talk about e-mail. Some of the words are new, and some of them are old words with new e-mail meanings.

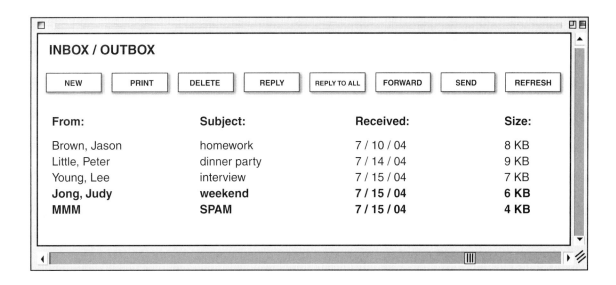

INBOX / OUTBOX

| NEW | PRINT | DELETE | REPLY | REPLY TO ALL | FORWARD | SEND | REFRESH |

From:	Subject:	Received:	Size:
Brown, Jason	homework	7 / 10 / 04	8 KB
Little, Peter	dinner party	7 / 14 / 04	9 KB
Young, Lee	interview	7 / 15 / 04	7 KB
Jong, Judy	**weekend**	**7 / 15 / 04**	**6 KB**
MMM	**SPAM**	**7 / 15 / 04**	**4 KB**

Work with a partner. Read the words and their definitions. Then practice using the words as you answer the questions about the e-mail screen on page 19 with your partner. The first one is done for you.

Word	Definition
mouse	the separate, handheld control for your computer
click on	use the mouse to choose something on the screen that you want the computer to do
highlighted	written in a different color so you can see it easily
close (v)	turn off a computer program
forward	send information that you have received to another person
receive	get an e-mail
delete	erase
inbox	the screen that lists the e-mails you have received
outbox	the screen that shows e-mails you have sent
open (v)	start a computer document or program
spam	unwanted e-mail that usually tries to sell you something

1. If you want to send a message back to Jason Brown, what do you do?

   Click on his name. Click on "Reply." Type your message. Click on "Send."

2. Lee sent some useful information about an interview. You want to have a copy of this information on paper. What do you do?

   _____

3. You want to send Peter's message to Judy because she is also coming to the dinner party. What is the quickest way to do this?

   _____

4. Jason's e-mail came last week, and you don't need it anymore. What do you do?

   _____

5. You have some new e-mail. Which e-mail is new and how do you know?

   _____

6. One of these new e-mails is from a company you don't know. They probably want to sell you something, but you are not interested. Which e-mail is it? How do you know this, and what do you do about it?

   _____

7. You need to e-mail your friend, Natalie, because you have a question about tonight's homework. What do you do?

   _____

8. You want to check that you sent the e-mail to Natalie correctly. What do you do?

   _____

Vocabulary Review

A. Choose the best word or words to complete each sentence.

log on	over-the-counter	virus	delete
borrow	frustrated	inbox	work out
expanded	syllabus		

1. You don't need a doctor's prescription to buy _____ medicine.

2. My computer is not working. It will not open my files. I think it must have a _____.

3. I don't understand this word. Can I _____ your dictionary, please? I left mine at home.

4. John felt very _____. He spent three hours painting his kitchen. When his wife came home, she told him it was the wrong color.

5. I need a password in order to _____ to my computer.

6. Sara's business _____ very quickly. She had to employ more people to help her.

7. When I get unwanted e-mail, I _____ it without reading it.

8. My doctor told me I should _____ more often. He said I should join a gym or go for a walk every day.

9. When I asked the teacher about the final test, she told me to read her _____. The information was on this paper.

10. When I checked my _____, I found I had twenty new e-mail messages.

B. Complete the sentences using your own words.

1. When I finish my English classes, I want to major in _____.

2. As I read, I highlight words I don't know so that _____.

3. The doctor gave me a prescription because _____.

4. I am allergic to dogs, so _____.

5. It's difficult being a single parent because _____.

6. John installed his new computer program, and then _____.

7. When my grandmother passed away, _____.

8. I need to refill my prescription because _____.

9. Hoang wanted his business to expand, so he _____.

10. The teenager dropped out of school because _____.

Expanding the Topic

Connecting Reading with Writing

A. Answer the questions in complete sentences. Use ideas and vocabulary you have learned in this chapter.

1. Write about two students you met in this class. What are their names? Where do they come from?

2. Katya Valenski is a pharmacist. Do you think this is a good job? Why or why not?

3. Do you think César González has a good job? Would you like to have this job? Why or why not?

4. Make a list of the good things about having your own business. Use Reading 3 to help you, but also think of some of your own ideas.

5. Make a list of the bad things about having your own business.

B. The first two readings describe the daily routine of Katya and César. What do you do on a normal weekday? Write a paragraph describing your daily routine.

Exploring Online

It is always a good idea to have a **buddy,** or friend, in your class. If you can't come to school one day, you can call or e-mail your buddy and ask about the homework. You can ask what happened in class. Take these steps:

1. Choose a buddy in your English class. Ask your buddy for his or her e-mail address. Write the name of your buddy and the address here.

   Name: _____

   E-mail: _____

2. If your buddy does not have an e-mail address, ask for a telephone number.

   Telephone: _____

3. Write an e-mail to your friend. Say that you missed class today because you were sick. Ask your buddy what happened in class. Ask if there is any homework. Send the e-mail.

4. Your buddy will reply to your e-mail. Print out the two messages and bring them to class to share with the other students. If your buddy does not have e-mail, call and ask for the same information.

From One Language to Another

wilkommen

benvenuto

Добро пожаловать

bienvenida

어서 오세요

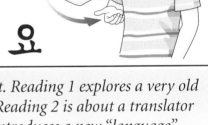

Chapter 2 is about languages past and present. Reading 1 explores a very old form of Egyptian writing called hieroglyphs. Reading 2 is about a translator who has an unusual boss. The third reading introduces a new "language" called text messaging.

In this chapter, you will practice:

Reading Skills

➡ Previewing a reading

➡ Finding reasons

➡ Understanding pronouns

Vocabulary Skills

➡ Previewing vocabulary

➡ Choosing the correct word form

Life Skills

➡ Finding information on the Internet

Writing of the Past

Before You Read

Previewing

Work with a partner. Discuss the questions and complete the tasks.

1. Look at the illustrations on pages 27 and 28. What do you think these pictures mean?

2. Look at the different languages written or signed on page 24. These words all mean "welcome." How many of these languages can you recognize?

3. Do you know any other words for "welcome"? What languages are they in? Write the words here:

   _____

   _____

   _____

   _____

4. "Welcome" is a greeting. What other greetings do you know in English? Write the greetings here:

   _____

   _____

   _____

   _____

5. This chapter is about translating from one language to another. What do you do when you don't understand something you are reading?

6. What do you say when you don't understand what someone is saying?

Previewing Vocabulary

These words are in Reading 1. Read the words and their definitions. Then choose the best word to complete each sentence.

Word	Definition
complicated	difficult to understand
columns	lines going from top to bottom
gradually	happening slowly
simple	easy to understand
archaeologists	people who study ancient societies
tomb	a place where a dead person is put
code	a system of words, letters, or signs that make a secret message
carvings	pictures or words that people cut into wood or stone

1. The past tense in English is very _____. I sometimes don't understand it because some verbs are regular and other verbs are irregular.

2. I am _____ learning how to speak English. Learning any language takes a long time.

3. Sometimes in a war, soldiers write messages in _____. They don't want the enemy to understand what they are writing.

4. When you begin to learn a language, you should write in _____ sentences. These sentences are easy to write and easy to understand.

5. _____ were very excited when they found the city of Pompeii. Dust and dirt covered this city for thousands of years.

6. You write English from left to right. You write Arabic from right to left. You write Chinese in _____ from top to bottom.

7. In ancient Egypt, people buried a king in a _____ when he died. They also put gold and money next to the dead king.

8. There were beautiful _____ on the stone wall. I could see pictures of birds and animals.

Now Read

Writing of the Past

1. One of the oldest forms of writing is from 3500 B.C. It is called hieroglyphic writing, and it was used in ancient Egypt. This form of writing used pictures and signs, called hieroglyphs, as letters and words. It was a very beautiful but complicated way of writing. In those days in Egypt, only a few people knew how to read and write. These people were known as scribes, and they worked for the kings of Egypt. Scribes spent many years learning how to read and write hieroglyphs because they were so complicated.

2. Hieroglyphic writing was complicated for several reasons. There were thousands of different signs. Sometimes the scribes wrote from right to left. Other times, they wrote from left to right. You can see which way to read by looking at the direction the animals are facing. For example, you should read the word on page 28 from right to left because the animals are facing left. Sometimes scribes even wrote in columns. They did not use punctuation or capital letters.

3. At first, scribes used burned wood to write on stone. Carvers then cut the hieroglyphs into the stone. Later, Egyptians discovered how to make paper. They made it out of papyrus, which is a kind of grass. After that, scribes could write directly on paper. They no longer needed carvers.

4. More people wanted to learn to read and write. They also wanted to write more quickly. So gradually people began to develop a new form of writing that was more simple. This writing was much easier to learn and to read than hieroglyphs were. As Egyptian writing changed, people forgot how to read and write hieroglyphs.

5. When archaeologists discovered hieroglyphs in the tombs of ancient Egyptian kings, they could not read them. They were like a secret code. Then in 1798, French soldiers in Egypt discovered a strange stone with carvings on it. The carvings looked like writing. The stone was black and about four feet long. People called it the Rosetta Stone. Historians studied it and found that there were three ancient kinds of writing on the stone. One of these was hieroglyphic writing. However, no one could understand what the hieroglyphs said.

[1] This says "welcome" in hieroglyphics.

continued

6   Then in 1822, a French historian studied the stone. He recognized that one of the languages on the stone was ancient Greek. He understood the Greek words. This helped him decipher, or figure out, the hieroglyphs. For the first time in thousands of years, people could understand and translate this ancient Egyptian form of writing.

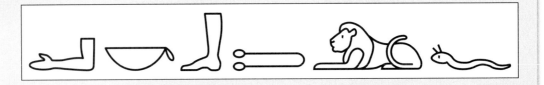

After You Read

How Well Did You Read?

Read the statements. Write *T* (true) or *F* (false). If there is not enough information in the reading to answer the question, write *N.*

_____ 1. Not many people in ancient Egypt could read or write.

_____ 2. Hieroglyphs were beautiful to look at and simple to read.

_____ 3. The Rosetta Stone helped historians understand hieroglyphs.

_____ 4. Scribes did not like writing in hieroglyphs.

Check Your Understanding

Circle the letter of the best answer.

1. *It is called hieroglyphic writing, and it was used in ancient Egypt.*
   This means _____.

   a. very old people wrote in hieroglyphs in Egypt
   b. people wrote in hieroglyphs in Egypt thousands of years ago
   c. hieroglyphs are still used by old people in Egypt today

2. Scribes were people who _____.

   a. discovered how to make paper from papyrus
   b. carved letters into stone
   c. knew how to read and write hieroglyphs

3. Why was papyrus better than stone to write on?

   a. Papyrus was stronger than stone.
   b. Scribes didn't need carvers to help them write their words.
   c. Papyrus was easy to carve so the scribes could do it themselves.

4. Why did hieroglyphic writing change to a different kind of writing?

   a. People wanted an easier and faster way to write.
   b. People in Egypt forgot how to write in hieroglyphs.
   c. The new writing was harder to learn than hieroglyphs were.

5. Why was the Rosetta Stone so important? The Rosetta Stone was very important because_____.

   a. it was over two thousand years old
   b. it helped historians learn how to read hieroglyphs
   c. it was the first thing French soldiers discovered in Egypt

6. *This helped him **decipher,** or figure out, the hieroglyphs.*
   Decipher means _____.

   a. to understand something that is complicated or written in secret code
   b. to tell the world about something
   c. to read and understand something in your language

7. A historian is a person who studies _____.

   a. languages
   b. the past
   c. Egypt

8. *For the first time in thousands of years, people could understand and **translate** this ancient Egyptian writing.*
   Translate means _____.

   a. to read and write in your language
   b. to decipher an ancient language
   c. to change one language into another language

Reading Skill

Finding Reasons

A *why* question asks you to give a reason or reasons for something. Look at questions 3, 4, and 5 on pages 28 and 29. These are all questions that ask "why?" When we answer, we often use *because* to introduce reasons.

Example:

Why did scribes spend many years learning how to read and write hieroglyphs?

because they were so complicated

Scribes took a long time to learn hieroglyphs *because* this form of writing was so complicated.

A. Read Reading 1 again to find answers to these *why* questions. Underline the answers in the reading. Then write these answers in the blanks using complete sentences. The first one is done for you.

1. Why was hieroglyphic writing so complicated?

   a. <u>It was complicated because there were thousands of different signs.</u>

   b. _____

   c. _____

2. Why did Egyptians stop using hieroglyphs?

   a. _____

   b. _____

   c. _____

3. Why was the Rosetta Stone so important?

   a. _____

   b. _____

   c. _____

B. Answer these questions about yourself. Give more than one reason for each question. Answer in complete sentences.

1. Why are you studying English?

   a. _____

   b. _____

   c. _____

2. Why is English sometimes a difficult language to learn?

   a. _____

   b. _____

   c. _____

3. Why do you think children learn English more quickly and easily than adults?

   a. _____

   b. _____

   c. _____

Understanding Pronouns

A **pronoun** is a word that replaces a noun or a noun phrase. *I, you, he, she, it, we, us, this,* and *these* are examples of pronouns. Writers use pronouns instead of repeating a noun. When you read, you need to understand which noun or noun phrase the pronoun is replacing.

Example:

Archaeologists discovered hieroglyphic writing in the tombs of Ancient Egyptian kings. However, they could not read **it**.

It refers to hieroglyphic writing.

If you don't understand a pronoun in a sentence, reread the sentence and the sentence before it to find the noun or noun phrase that the pronoun is replacing.

A. Look at the pronoun in bold print. Underline the noun or noun phrase that the pronoun is replacing.

1. <u>One of the oldest forms of writing</u> we know about was used in 3500 B.C. **It** is called hieroglyphic writing.

2. Scribes spent years learning how to read and write hieroglyphs because **they** were so complicated.

3. Sometimes the scribes wrote from right to left. Other times, **they** wrote from left to right.

4. Scribes wrote about kings and rules. **They** also wrote about their gods and government.

5. Later, they used an easier form called demotic writing. **This** was much easier than hieroglyphic writing.

B. Complete the sentences with the correct pronoun.

1. Historians and archaeologists knew the writing on the Rosetta Stone was from Ancient Egypt. However, _____ couldn't understand it.

2. The writing on the Rosetta Stone was about young King Ptolemy V. _____ was only thirteen when he became king.

continued

3. If my classmates and I want to find a translation of the Rosetta Stone, _____ can look online or go to the library.

4. The Rosetta Stone is now in a museum in London. Thousands of people go to see _____ each year.

5. When Egyptian kings died, they were buried with a special book. _____ was called the Book of the Dead.

Interpreting for the "Little Giant"

Before You Read

Previewing

Work in small groups. Discuss the questions.

1. Look at the photo on page 33. Describe the people in the photo. What sport do you think the tallest man plays?

2. The tallest man is Chinese. He plays for a team in the United States. Can you think of any other players or athletes who have gone to the U.S.A. to play a sport? How do you think these players communicate when they first arrive?

3. Do you sometimes need help in speaking or understanding English? Who helps you translate from your language to English? Do you help translate for anyone?

Previewing Vocabulary

These words are in Reading 2. Read the words and their definitions. Then choose the best word or words to complete each sentence.

Word	Definition
bilingual	able to speak two languages very well
fluent	able to speak a language very well
famous	known about and admired by a lot of people
coach	someone who trains a sports team
terms	special words or phrases for a specific subject
run errands	do the small jobs of daily life such as shopping or mailing a letter

1. I started to learn Spanish two years ago. I am not _____, but I can speak it quite well.

2. I have to _____ for my boss. He sends me to other offices to deliver messages. Sometimes I go downtown and buy things for him.

3. David Beckham is a _____ soccer player. People all around the world watch him play.

4. The football _____ made the players work very hard. He wanted them to be the best team.

5. I don't play basketball, so I don't understand basketball _____. For example, what does "slam dunk" mean?

6. My parents are Canadian, but they grew up in France. As a result, they are both _____. Sometimes we speak French in our family, and sometimes we speak English.

Now Read

Interpreting for the "Little Giant"

1   Colin Pine used to work in Washington, D.C. Pine is bilingual—he speaks Chinese and English. Before he worked in Washington, he lived and worked in Taiwan for several years. He became fluent in Chinese while he was living there. He loved living in Taiwan, and he loves speaking Chinese.

2   When Pine returned to America, he got a job with the State Department in Washington, D.C. He translated Chinese newspapers into English. It was a good job, but not very interesting. Pine was thinking about a new career. What would be an interesting job?

3   A friend showed him an advertisement for a job. It said a famous basketball team was looking for an interpreter to work with a new

continued

---

basketball player from China. The basketball player did not speak very good English. "Why don't you apply, Colin?" asked his friend.

4   Colin didn't have to think about this for very long. He loved two things in life: Chinese and basketball. This job sounded perfect! So he applied for the job. He didn't think he would get the job because he knew many people wanted to work with a famous basketball team.

5   Although the ad did not give the name of the Chinese player, Pine guessed who it was. It was no secret that Yao Ming from Shanghai was joining the Houston Rockets basketball team. Pine liked this team very much. His favorite player, Steve Francis, played for the Rockets. Pine wrote about this in his application.

6   To his surprise, Pine got a phone call from Yao Ming's cousin, Erik Zhang. Zhang asked him to translate from Chinese to English, and from English to Chinese, on the phone. They also talked about basketball. Pine got the job and was soon on a plane to meet his new boss.

7   And what a boss! Yao Ming's parents both played for China's national basketball teams. His mother is 6'3" and his father is 6'7". Their "little" boy was 6'6" when he was twelve years old. He is now 7'5" —one of the tallest basketball players in the world. People in China call him the Little Giant. Pine, by the way, is about 5'10".[1]

[1] Source: usatoday.com 2002

8   Colin Pine is Yao Ming's interpreter. An interpreter translates the words spoken in one language into a different language. When Yao Ming's basketball coach tells him to do something in the game, Pine translates the instructions into Chinese. When reporters interview Yao Ming, Pine translates their questions and Yao's answers.

9   Interpreting is a very difficult job. You must be fluent in two languages. You must be able to think very quickly. You must be able to translate one part of the sentence while you are listening to the next part of the sentence. You must also understand the subject you are translating—in Pine's case, basketball. Pine must accurately translate basketball terms into Chinese.

10   Interpreting is the most important part of Pine's job, but he has other

continued

responsibilities, too. He runs errands for Yao. He also helps Yao learn about American culture and customs. He taught him to drive, and he was very proud when Yao passed his driver's test. He spends most days and evenings with his boss. In fact, Pine lives with Yao and his mother in Houston. They have become good friends.

11 Yao learned English in Shanghai, so he spoke a little English when he arrived in the United States. Pine is helping him improve his English, and Yao is a good student. One day in the future, Yao Ming will not need an interpreter, but he will always need a friend.

After You Read

How Well Did You Read?

Read the statements. Write *T* (true), *F* (false), or *N* (not enough information).

_____ 1. Pine applied for this job as an interpreter because he enjoyed speaking Chinese and watching basketball.

_____ 2. Yao Ming was the first successful basketball player in his family.

_____ 3. A good interpreter can do several things at the same time.

_____ 4. Next year, Yao Ming will not need Pine as an interpreter.

Check Your Understanding

A. Circle the letter of the best answer.

1. Why was Colin Pine thinking about a new job while he was working in Washington, D.C.?

    a. He wanted to return to Taiwan.
    b. His job was not very interesting.
    c. He wanted to play basketball.

2. Which statement is correct according to the reading?

    a. Pine lived in Washington, D.C., before he lived in Taiwan.
    b. Pine was working in Taiwan when he heard about the job with Yao Ming.
    c. Pine lived and worked in Taiwan before he lived in Washington, D.C.

3. Pine guessed the Chinese player was Yao Ming because _____.

    a. Erik Zhang, Yao's cousin, called him and told him
    b. he knew Yao Ming was joining an American basketball team
    c. his favorite player, Steve Francis, told him

continued

4. It is important for Yao Ming's interpreter to understand basketball because
   _____.

   a. he has to coach Yao and the other players in basketball
   b. he has to think and speak very quickly
   c. he has to understand basketball terms in order to translate them

5. *When Yao Ming's basketball coach tells **him** to do something in the game, Pine translates the instructions into Chinese.*

   Him refers to _____.

   a. Yao Ming
   b. the basketball coach
   c. Colin Pine

6. *"Why don't you **apply**, Colin?" asked his friend.*

   Apply means to _____.

   a. find out more about a job
   b. try to get a new job
   c. look for a new job

7. Good interpreters must _____.

   a. be bilingual
   b. think slowly and carefully before they speak
   c. run errands for the boss

8. Pine thinks the most important part of his job is _____.

   a. to interpret for Yao
   b. to help Yao in his daily life
   c. to teach Yao to drive

9. *Although the advertisement did not give the name of the Chinese player, Pine guessed who **it** was.*

   It refers to _____.

   a. the name of the Chinese player
   b. Colin Pine
   c. the application

10. In the future, Yao Ming will not need an interpreter because _____.

    a. he already speaks English well
    b. he will speak and understand English well
    c. he will always have Pine as a friend

B. Read about Colin Pine and Yao Ming again. Underline the answers to each question as you read. Then write the answers in the blanks.

1. Why did Pine want to work as an interpreter for Yao?

   a. _____

   b. _____

   c. _____

2. Why is interpreting a difficult job?

   a. _____

   b. _____

   c. _____

   d. _____

Vocabulary Skill

Choosing the Correct Word Form

A word often belongs to a word family. In its family, the word often has different forms, depending on the part of speech. The word family usually has a verb, noun, and adjective. Understanding the word form will help you understand the reading.

Examples:

Verb	Noun	Adjective
instruct	instruction	instructional
agree	agreement	agreeable

A. Reading 2 uses one or more words from each of these word families. Find which words are in the reading and underline them in the list.

Verb	Noun
apply	application / applicant
advertise	advertisement (ad)
interpret	interpretation / interpreter
play	player

B. Choose a word from the list to complete the sentences. If you use a verb, make sure to use the correct form.

1. Pine's friend saw the _____ in the newspaper about this job.

2. Although Pine doesn't _____ basketball, he loves watching the games.

3. Colin Pine wrote a letter to _____ for the job. Luckily, his _____ was successful, and he got the job.

4. Yao Ming's coach needed an _____ who understood Chinese and basketball. He wanted someone to _____ his instructions quickly and accurately.

Text Messaging: A New Language?

Before You Read

Previewing

Work in small groups. Discuss the questions and complete the tasks.

1. Look at the photo on this page. What are these people doing?

2. How do you communicate with a friend who lives in a different city? Make a list of the different ways you can communicate with people.

   _____
   _____
   _____
   _____

3. Try to read the sentence under the title of Reading 3 on page 39. Can you understand it? What language is it in?

Previewing Vocabulary

These words are in Reading 3. Read the words and their definitions. Then choose the best word or words to complete each sentence.

Word	Definition
generally	usually
keys	the numbers and letters you use on a phone or computer
local calls	phone calls to someone who lives nearby
cell phone/mobile phone	a phone you carry with you that works by receiving wireless signals
popular	liked by a lot of people

1. When I ran out of gas on the freeway, I had my _____ with me. I called my friend and asked him to help me.

2. Maria took a typing class in high school. Now when she types, she doesn't have to look at the _____. She can type very quickly.

3. My mother only lives a few miles away. I call her every night. It doesn't cost anything because _____ are free.

4. I _____ do my grocery shopping on weekends. Sometimes, however, I need something and have to go to the grocery store on weekdays.

5. Gloria Estefan is a very _____ Latino pop singer. Many people all over the world love her music.

Now Read

Text Messaging: A New Language?

I CNT SPK 2 U. I AM L8 4 DNR. TLK2UL8TR. BFN.

1   To some people, text messaging looks as complicated as hieroglyphs. To the millions of people who use it, however, text messaging is a simple, quick, and cheap way to communicate with friends. These people can easily translate the message above. It says, "I can't speak to you. I'm late for dinner. Talk to you later. Bye for now."

continued

2   Text messaging means sending short messages from one cell phone to another. You send a message by using the keys on your phone. The message arrives very quickly—usually in a few seconds. The phone's screen displays the message.

3   Text messages usually have up to 160 characters or letters. A message this short is very cheap. Longer messages cost more. It is difficult to write a message using only 160 characters. So, to keep the cost down, users developed a short form of writing. They use a few letters and numbers to represent phrases and words. Here are some examples of these new "words":

B/F	boyfriend	IC	I see
BC	because	ILU	I love you
B4	before	JK	just kidding (joking)
BFN	bye for now	NOYB	none of your business
CU	see you	OTB	off to bed
CUL8R	see you later	SUP	What's up? What's happening?
G/F	girlfriend		
G2R	got to run (I must go)	TTYS	talk to you soon
GL	good luck	WAN2TLK	Do you want to talk?
LOL	laughing out loud	YW	You're welcome.

4   Text messaging also uses these symbols to show how the writer is feeling:

:-)	happy	:-O	surprised
:-))	very happy	:-ll	angry
:-(	sad	%-)	confused

5   Text messaging is very popular in Europe, especially with people twelve to thirty-four years old. In fact, Europeans send about ten billion text messages a month. Any visitor to London, Paris, or Berlin will discover that this new form of communication is very popular. People on trains and buses, in stores, and even at work will be busy using their fingers and their mobile phones to "talk" to their friends.

6   Text messaging is not as popular in the United States, although the number of people using text messaging is growing. In June 2001, Americans sent thirty million messages. In June of the following year, they sent one billion messages. That was not very many compared with Europe. There are several reasons why text messaging is not as popular in the United States. Phone calls are cheaper than in Europe. Most local calls in the U.S. are free. People prefer to talk on the phone. Also, Internet services in the United States are cheap. More people use e-mail to communicate. Using e-mail is much easier than using text messaging because people can use ordinary words. They can also send long messages. Finally, text messaging is more expensive in America than in Europe.

continued

7   While millions use this form of language to communicate, some parents believe text messaging is bad for children and students. They think that students will use text messaging "words" in their schoolwork. They believe students will forget how to write well and will make more mistakes in spelling and grammar. Teachers in Europe, however, do not think that students make more mistakes because of text messaging. In fact, many teachers like it because students are writing more and enjoying their writing. Teachers believe students know that text language can only be used in messaging. It is like a secret code, and teenagers do not want to share it with adults. So they do not generally use it in the classroom.

8   Languages change all the time. New words are added as old words are forgotten. Text messaging is an example of how technology has changed a language very quickly. It may seem new to some people, but, like hieroglyphs, it is just another way of using letters and signs to communicate. So, CUL8R!

After You Read

How Well Did You Read?

Read the statements. Write *T* (true), *F* (false), or *N* (not enough information).

_____ 1. You need a computer to send a text message.

_____ 2. People in Paris like text messaging more than people in Berlin.

_____ 3. Text messaging is less popular in America than in Europe.

_____ 4. Text messaging is an example of how a language can change.

Check Your Understanding

A. Answer the questions in complete sentences.

1. Why do some people think text messaging is like hieroglyphs?

   <u>They think text messaging is like hieroglyphs because both are</u>

   <u>complicated to read.</u>

2. What is text messaging?

   _____

   _____

continued

3. How long can a text message usually be?

_____

_____

4. Why did people begin to use short text "words"?

_____

_____

5. If a person is feeling unhappy and wants to talk to a friend, what could they send as a text message?

_____

_____

6. What will visitors to a large European city see?

_____

_____

7. How would you write the following message in text messaging? *I have to go because I'm late. I love you, and I'll call you later.*

_____

_____

8. How many text messages did Americans send in June 2002?

_____

_____

9. Why do some parents worry about text messaging?

_____

_____

10. Do you think text messaging will change in the future? Why or why not?

_____

_____

B. Read the story about text messaging again. Underline the answers to each question as you read. Then write the answers in the blanks. Use short answers.

1. Why is text messaging not very popular in the United States?

   a. _____

   b. _____

   c. _____

2. Why aren't teachers worried about text messaging?

   a. _____

   b. _____

   c. _____

3. How do languages change?

   a. _____

   b. _____

Vocabulary Review

A. Choose the best word to complete each sentence.

ancient	translate	secret	sign
discovered	complicated	direction	simple
gradually	archaeologists		

1. Which _____ is the wind blowing? Is it from the north or the south?

2. The traffic _____ for stop in my country is a large red circle with the letter S in the middle.

3. Historians study tombs of the _____ Egyptian kings. They have found out a lot about how people lived.

4. I don't understand Japanese. You speak both Japanese and English. Could you _____ for me, please?

continued

5. When I first started college, math was _____, but now it is a lot more difficult. Sometimes it is very hard to understand.

6. The boy was not very good at playing the piano at first. However, he kept trying and he _____ became better. Now he is very good.

7. I can't tell you. It is a _____. I am not allowed to tell anyone.

8. The builders _____ some very old pots. They didn't know what they were, so they asked archaeologists to come and take a look.

9. Math and science are easy for me. However, learning a second language is very _____. I don't understand the grammar, and there are too many new words to learn!

10. _____ find out about the past by looking at very old things.

B. Complete the sentences using your own words.

1. The Spanish actor needed an interpreter because _____.

2. I applied for the job, but _____.

3. If you want to be fluent in a language you must _____.

4. You can use the keys on your cell phone to _____.

5. When you make a local call, you don't need to _____.

6. I have to run an errand. My mom wants me to _____.

7. The student completed the application and _____.

8. My English teacher is very popular because _____.

9. It is good to be bilingual because _____.

10. I saw an advertisement that said "_____."

Expanding the Topic

Connecting Reading with Writing

A. Answer the questions in complete sentences. Use information and vocabulary you have learned in this chapter.

1. What is the most difficult thing about learning English for you?

2. What do you think is the best way to learn English? Why?

3. Is it more difficult to speak English inside your English classroom or outside the classroom? Explain your answer.

B. Choose one of the following topics and write a paragraph. Use the readings to help you, but try to make your own sentences.

1. **Hieroglyphs.** What are hieroglyphs? When and where did people use hieroglyphic writing? How do people understand this writing today? Begin your paragraph:

   Hieroglyphs are

2. **Colin Pine and Yao Ming.** Do you think Colin Pine was a good choice for the job of interpreter for Yao Ming? Give several reasons for your opinion. Begin your paragraph:

   I think Colin Pine was a good (not a good) choice as an interpreter

   for several reasons. First,

3. **Communication today.** Think of all the different ways we can communicate today. How do you communicate with people who live far away from you? What is the best way to communicate with someone who lives in a different country? Begin your paragraph:

   Today we can communicate with people in many ways.

Exploring Online

Life Skill

Finding Information on the Internet

Today, we can find information quickly and easily on the Internet. The World Wide Web, or simply the Web, has information about every subject you can think of.

A book organizes information into chapters. On the Internet, information is organized in Web sites. There are billions of Web sites. To find these sites, we use a search engine. Here are some examples of search engines:

www.google.com
www.yahoo.com
www.msn.com

A. You need to find a pharmacy near your house. You want to know what time it opens and where it is.

1. Log on to your computer and choose a search engine.

2. Type the name of a major pharmacy in the search box. Examples are Rite Aid, Walgreens, Fred Meyers, and Safeway. Press Search.

continued

3. The screen will have a list of Web sites about the pharmacy you chose. The home page of that pharmacy is usually one of the first Web sites on the list of search results. Look for the address, for example: www.walgreens.com. Click on the link to the home page.

4. Now look for the "Find a store" or "Locate a store" link on the pharmacy's home page. Click on it. The screen will ask you for a city and state or a zip code. Enter this information and press Search.

5. You will now have a list of stores near your house.

B. Use the information from the Web site to fill in the blanks.

The pharmacy I chose is _____ (name of pharmacy).

Its hours are _____.

The address is _____.

C. Many Web sites for businesses have maps to help you find the business. Look for the map link for the pharmacy you chose. Click on it and print a copy of the map. Bring it to class.

D. Form small groups. Using the map to help you, explain to your group how to get to the pharmacy from your house.

"Home Sweet Home"

The third chapter is about homes. In Reading 1, you will read about international students who are living with host families. Reading 2 is about two students who are trying to find an apartment. Reading 3 is about people who have no home: the homeless.

In this chapter, you will practice:

Reading Skills

➡ Previewing a reading

➡ Predicting

Vocabulary Skills

➡ Previewing vocabulary

➡ Using context clues to understand vocabulary

➡ Understanding phrasal verbs with *get*

Life Skills

➡ Reading numbers out loud

➡ Understanding housing abbreviations

➡ Finding information on the Internet

Before You Read

Previewing

Discuss the questions with a partner.

1. The title of this chapter is "Home Sweet Home." What do you think it means?

2. Look at the photos on page 47. What kind of house do you live in?

3. Read the title of Reading 1. What do you think this reading is going to be about?

4. An international student is a student who comes to a country to study. International students have a student visa and cannot work. They will return to their home country when they finish college. A resident student is a student who comes to America to live for a long time. The resident student can work and usually plans to stay in the country where he or she is living and working. Are you a resident student or an international student?

Previewing Vocabulary

These words are in Reading 1. Read the words and their definitions. Then choose the best word or words to complete each sentence.

Word	Definition
room and board	a room to sleep in and meals
culture	art, ideas, behavior, and beliefs of a society or group of people
bus line	the route a bus takes
rule	an instruction that says how you must do something and what you are allowed to do
participate	take part in an activity
miss	not go somewhere or not do something
communication	talking or writing to each other

1. I decided to stay at the Starlight Hotel because _____ was only fifty dollars a day.

2. Most colleges have the _____ that students may not smoke in the classroom.

3. At first, many students from other countries do not understand American _____. For example, Americans behave and think quite differently than people from Japan.

4. My house is in a very good place. It is on the _____ to school, so I don't need to drive and I don't have to worry about parking.

5. "I'm sorry, but I will _____ class tomorrow. I have a doctor's appointment."

6. "You must _____ in class," said the teacher. "I want you all to talk in your groups and ask lots of questions."

7. In American classes, _____ between the students and the teacher is very important. Everyone must talk to each other so they get to know each other.

Now Read

Living with a Host Family

1   Each year, over half a million students leave their native countries to study English in America. Many international students decide to live with a host family while they are studying in America. A host family offers room and board to international students. There are a lot of advantages to living with a host family, so each year thousands of students choose to stay with one.

2   One advantage is that host families help students when they arrive. The families meet students at the airport and drive them to their new homes. They show the students how to get to school and help them understand the bus lines. Another advantage is the cost. It is usually cheaper to stay with a family than to live in an apartment. The cost of room and board with host families varies from city to city. In New York, for example, room and board is more expensive than in Oklahoma. The biggest advantage to living with a host family is that students can experience American culture and improve their English. Students participate in daily activities with the family. They eat meals together and go grocery shopping. They get to know about American lifestyles, and while they are doing this, they are speaking and improving their English.

3   Students usually enjoy their stay with a host family. However, sometimes there are problems. These problems are usually because of cultural misunderstandings. Something that is acceptable in one culture may not be okay in another culture. For example, a student from Ghana was always late for the family dinner. In her culture, it was rude to be early or on time, but in American culture, it is not polite to be late. A Japanese student was shocked to find that the family's pet dog lived inside the house. It sometimes slept on his bed. Even worse to him, the family washed the dog dish in the dishwasher with the other dishes. Finally, a host family with an

continued

Indonesian student thought he was rude because he didn't help with any housework. These are examples of cultural misunderstanding.

4   What can a student do to prevent problems? It is very important to ask questions. In American culture, it is good to ask questions. Students should ask questions about family rules. It is important to know about these. You need to understand what you can and cannot do in your new family. Some good questions are:

- What should I call you?
- What time is dinner?
- What time does the family go to bed?
- Can I watch TV after the family goes to bed?
- Can I use the telephone for local calls? Can I make long-distance calls?
- Can I bring my friends home? Can they come in my bedroom?

5   It is also acceptable to ask your host family to explain something again if you don't understand the first time. If you are not sure, it is always better to ask. You can ask politely:

- Excuse me. I don't understand. Can you repeat that?
- I'm sorry. I don't understand. Can you write it down for me?

6   Finally, you need to keep your host family informed. You must tell them if you have any food allergies. You should also tell them if you don't like certain foods. Make sure you let them know if you will miss dinner, or if you are going away for the weekend. If you have a problem, talk about it. The most important part of any friendship is communication. So don't be shy—communicate and enjoy your stay!

After You Read

How Well Did You Read?

Work with a partner. Read the statements. Write *T* (true) or *F* (false).

_____ **1.** An international student comes to this country to get a job.

_____ **2.** A host family cooks meals for the student who is staying with the family.

_____ **3.** Students usually need a car if they live with a host family.

_____ **4.** If students don't understand something, they should keep quiet.

Discussing the Reading

Work with a partner. Talk about the questions.

1. Do you live in a house, an apartment, or with a host family? Do you like where you live? Why or why not?

2. What are some of the good things about living with a host family according to the reading? Can you think of any other good things about living with a host family?

3. What questions should the student ask according to the reading? Can you think of any more good questions?

4. This reading says that living in an apartment is more expensive than living with a host family. Do you agree? Explain your answer to the group.

5. What are the examples of cultural misunderstandings in the reading? Have you experienced any cultural misunderstandings?

Check Your Understanding

Circle the letter of the best answer.

1. Why do many students choose to live with a host family?

   a. Staying with a host family is more expensive than staying in an apartment.
   b. There are a lot of good reasons to stay with a host family.
   c. Students leave their countries to learn English.

2. Which statement is correct?

   a. Students must have a car when they live with a host family.
   b. The cost of room and board with a host family is the same in every city.
   c. Students learn about American culture when they stay with a host family.

3. *A Japanese student was shocked to find that the family's pet dog lived inside the house. It sometimes slept on his bed. Even worse to him, the family washed the dog dish in the dishwasher with the other dishes.*

   This is an example of

   a. a bad dog.
   b. a cultural misunderstanding.
   c. a dirty family.

4. *Students should ask questions about family rules. It is important to know about **these**.*

   These refers to

   a. students.
   b. questions.
   c. rules.

continued

5. Why is it polite to ask questions in American culture?

    a. because asking for information helps prevent problems
    b. because asking questions helps students improve their English
    c. because people like to talk

<table>
<tr><td>

Vocabulary Skill

</td><td>

Using Context Clues to Understand Vocabulary

You don't need to use your dictionary for every word you don't understand. Often you can guess the meaning by carefully reading the other words in the sentence. The other words and sentences around the new word are the **context.** Guessing the meaning of vocabulary through context is an important reading skill. It increases your vocabulary and helps you read faster.

For example, look at this sentence:

    I love ice cream, but I **detest** yogurt. If I eat it, I get sick.

If you don't know the word *detest,* you can guess its meaning by looking at the words around it—the context. This person loves ice cream, but detests yogurt. The word *but* tells you *detest* is the opposite of *love.* Also, if this person eats yogurt, he gets sick. So, you can guess that *detest* refers to something bad. *Detest* must mean "hate."

</td></tr>
</table>

A. Read these sentences carefully. Guess the meaning of the words in bold print by looking at the context. Circle the letter of the best answer.

1. When I moved in with my host family, my host mother gave me a **contract.** She told me to read it carefully. The contract said how much I would pay each month and when I must pay. It also said I was not allowed to smoke in my bedroom. After I read it, I signed it. My host mother also wrote her name on the contract.

    a. a rule
    b. a written agreement between two people
    c. a credit card bill

2. Living in a new culture can be **confusing.** Sometimes I don't understand the people here.

    a. easy to understand
    b. difficult to understand
    c. unhappy

3. My host mother is a single parent. She has a **toddler** who is just learning to walk. He's cute!

    a. young brother
    b. daughter
    c. one- to three-year-old child

4. "You must be **punctual**," said the teacher. "If you are late, I will give you extra homework."

   a. very late
   b. on time
   c. quiet

B. Work with a partner. Read these sentences from Reading 1. Guess the meaning of the words in bold print by looking at the context. Circle the letter of the best answer.

1. *There are a lot of **advantages** to living with a host family, so each year thousands of students choose to stay with one.*

   a. good things that help you
   b. bad things that don't help you
   c. problems

2. *Another advantage is the **cost**. It is usually cheaper to stay with a family than to live in an apartment.*

   a. comfort
   b. how much something is
   c. money

3. *The cost of room and board with host families **varies** from city to city. In New York, for example, room and board is more expensive than in Oklahoma.*

   a. stays the same
   b. doesn't change
   c. changes

4. *For example, a student from Ghana was always late for the family dinner. In her culture, it was **rude** to be early or on time, but in American culture, it is not polite to be late.*

   a. polite
   b. not polite
   c. okay

5. *Something that is **acceptable** in one culture may not be okay in another culture.*

   a. okay
   b. not okay
   c. difficult

Reading Numbers Out Loud

Saying numbers correctly is important. In English, we say numbers like this:

10	ten
24	twenty-four
136	one hundred and thirty-six
4,892	four thousand, eight hundred and ninety-two
5,900	five thousand, nine hundred
175,602	one hundred and seventy-five thousand, six hundred and two
1,352,921	one million, three hundred and fifty-two thousand, nine hundred and twenty-one

Note that when the number is above a hundred, we usually say *and* before the last number.

A. Work with a partner. Look at the following table.

Which Countries Do International Students in America Come From?

Rank	Country	2000/1	2001/2
	World total	547,867	582,996
1 (first)	India	54,664	66,836
2 (second)	China	59,939	63,211
3 (third)	South Korea	45,685	49,046
4 (fourth)	Japan	46,497	46,810
5 (fifth)	Taiwan	28,566	28,930
6 (sixth)	Canada	25,279	26,514
7 (seventh)	Mexico	10,670	12,518
8 (eighth)	Turkey	10,983	12,091
9 (ninth)	Indonesia	11,625	11,614
10 (tenth)	Thailand	11,187	11,606

Source: Institute of International Education www.opendoors.iinetwork.org 2003

B. Practice asking and answering these questions with your partner.

1. How many international students came to the United States in 2000/1?

2. How many more came the next year?

3. Which country sent the most students in 2001/2? How many students came from this country in 2001/2?

4. How many students came from Taiwan in 2000/1?

5. Which country had a smaller number of students in 2001/2 than in 2000/1?

6. The number of international students from India grew by 22.3% (twenty-two point three percent). How many more students came in 2001/2 than in 2000/1?

7. How many international students in 2001/2 came from countries that are next to the United States?

C. Work with a partner. Student A reads the number aloud. Student B listens to the number, but doesn't look at it. Student B writes down the number he/she hears on a piece of paper. Take turns reading and writing.

1. 1,546,738

2. 573

3. 870,429

4. 2,900,461

5. 497,002

6. 5,988,300

7. 456

8. 444,442

9. 9,000,057

10. 356,111

Reading 2 *Part A: Finding an Apartment*

Before You Read

Previewing

Work in small groups. Discuss the questions.

1. Who in your group lives in an apartment? How did he or she find it?

2. What are some advantages to living in an apartment?

3. What are some disadvantages (bad things) about living in an apartment?

Using Context Clues to Understand Vocabulary

The words in bold print are in Reading 2, Part A. Guess the meaning of the words by looking at the context. Circle the letter of the best answer.

1. My brother is very friendly. He **gets along** with everyone. He has a lot of friends.

   a. is shy
   b. is friendly
   c. fights

2. When you need to buy something, you can look in the **classified section** of your newspaper. There are advertisements for everything—from pets to cars to houses.

   a. part of the paper that lists things for sale
   b. advertisements in a newspaper
   c. TV guide

3. Hiro **cannot afford** a new car yet. He needs to save some more money.

   a. can't drive
   b. doesn't have enough money for
   c. needs to borrow money for

4. There are too many students in this class. The **maximum** number of students is 25. We have 31. We will divide the class into two classes.

   a. highest
   b. lowest
   c. best

5. Claudia is a **resident** student of English. She is living in the U.S. and does not plan to return to her native country, Brazil, to live. She has a Green Card and is working in a childcare center.

   a. someone who is allowed to live and work in a country
   b. someone who comes to a country as an international student
   c. someone who is studying to improve his or her English

Life Skill

Understanding Housing Abbreviations

People advertise houses or apartments for rent in the newspaper. It is expensive to advertise. So advertisements are usually very short. We use abbreviations (letters or short words) in advertisements. Some common abbreviations are:

ba *or* bath:	bathroom
bed *or* bdrm	bedroom
NS	no smokers
1st last + dep	when you move in, you must pay the first and last month's rent plus a deposit
W/D	washer and dryer
ref req	references required

Now Read

Finding an Apartment

1   Peter is a resident student at Somerset Community College. He came to America several years ago because of the war in his country. America is now his home. He's taking English, math, and computer classes at the college as well as working at a local electronics company. He has lived with his uncle's family since he arrived in the States. Now, however, he wants to get his own apartment. He cannot afford to live by himself because renting an apartment is very expensive. So he is looking for a roommate. He decides to ask a classmate, Shinya, to share an apartment with him.

2   Shinya is an international student from Japan. He is living with a host family. He has lived with this family for a year. He gets along very well with the family, and they have become good friends. However, Shinya is now ready to be independent. He wants to live by himself or with a friend. When Peter asks him to share, Shinya is very happy. He definitely wants to move into an apartment with his friend.

3   Before they begin to look for an apartment, Peter and Shinya make a list of what they can afford and what they need.

rent: $350 each per month maximum

2 bedrooms

fireplace (Shinya likes to sit in front of a warm fire in the evening.)

continued

no pets in the building (Peter is allergic to animals.)

close to stores and college

covered parking (Peter likes to look after his car.)

on the bus line (Shinya doesn't have a car.)

must allow smoking (Shinya smokes.)

4   The two friends look at the classified section of the local paper. They find the following advertisements for two-bedroom apartments.

---

1. 2 bdrm/1 ba large kitchen clean new carpet. W/D. Good street parking. $550 1st, last + dep. Small pets OK. (113) 123-5432 Ref req.

2. 2 bdrm–1 bath apt. 1000 sq ft. Nice living room w/fireplace. Wood floors. Close to shops/bus line. W/D. Underground parking. $600 1st, last + dep. (445) 111-2233

3. 2 bed/2 bath. Large clean living space. Quiet country setting. Huge 2-acre lot. Horses OK. NS. $650 + dep. (445) 189-0001

4. Quiet, sunny 2 bdrm/1½ bath. New paint and carpet. Nice living room w/fireplace + cable TV. Private patio. Convenient location for shops/bus. Gas heat. Covered parking. Pool. $700 1st, last + $500 dep. Ref req. (113) 332-7767 evenings.

After You Read

How Well Did You Read?

Read the statements. Write *T* (true) or *F* (false).

_____ 1. Peter came to America to improve his English.

_____ 2. Shinya wants to move because he has problems with his host family.

_____ 3. They both need an apartment on a bus line.

_____ 4. The most they can pay together is $700 a month.

Predicting

Predicting means guessing what will happen before it happens. Predicting is an important part of reading. As you read, you try to predict, or guess, what the writer is going to say. This makes you think carefully about what you are reading. Predicting will help you understand more of the reading.

A. Complete this chart using the information about Peter and Shinya from Reading 2, Part A. Write the good points about each apartment under Advantages. Write the bad points under Disadvantages. You do not need to write complete sentences.

Apartment	Advantages	Disadvantages
1	cheap rent	pets are allowed
2		
3		
4		

B. Work in small groups. Discuss these questions.

1. Is apartment 1 a good choice for Peter and Shinya? Why or why not?

2. Is apartment 2 a good choice for Peter and Shinya? Why or why not?

3. Is apartment 3 a good choice for Peter and Shinya? Why or why not?

4. Is apartment 4 a good choice for Peter and Shinya? Why or why not?

C. Using the information from the chart, predict which apartment you think the two students will choose. Then give your reasons in a paragraph. Begin with this sentence:

I think Peter and Shinya will choose apartment _____. There are several reasons why they will choose this apartment. First, _____

_____.

Second, _____

_____ Next, _____

_____

_____

Finally, _____.

Vocabulary Skill

Understanding Phrasal Verbs with **Get**

Reading 2, Part A uses the phrasal verb *get along with.* This means to be friendly with someone. Here are some more phrasal verbs using *get:*

get away with	not be punished when you have done something wrong
get behind	be late doing something
get by	have enough money to buy what you need, but not more
get down to	finally start doing something that you didn't want to do
get off	finish work
get over	be healthy again after an illness
get rid of	make someone or something go away
get together	meet one or more people

Complete each sentence with the best phrasal verb from the list. Use the past tense.

1. John lost his job two months ago. Because he lost his job, he _____ on his rent. He needs to pay two months' rent, but he doesn't have the money. He is going to ask his parents for help.

2. I had a garage sale last week. People bought almost everything! I _____ a lot of things I didn't want.

3. Maria worked really hard yesterday because the woman who worked with her was sick. When Maria finally _____ work at 11:00 p.m., she was very tired.

4. During the war, some people _____ doing very bad things. They were not punished after the war.

5. Pham finally _____ her homework just before midnight. She didn't want to do it earlier.

6. My husband caught SARS last year when he was in Hong Kong. He _____ it, but he was sick for a long time.

7. Last night, several students from the class _____ to talk about their homework. They finished the homework, ordered a pizza, and had a great time talking with each other.

8. My mother was a single parent. She _____ with very little money. Life was difficult, but my sisters and I were never hungry.

Reading 2 | *Part B: Moving In*

Now Read

In Reading 2, Part A, Peter and Shinya were looking at advertisements for an apartment. Read the rest of the story without stopping. If you don't understand a word, try to guess its meaning from the context.

Moving In

1   Peter and Shinya decided to look at two of the apartments. They looked at the apartment that was $600 a month, and the apartment that was $700 a month. First they telephoned and made appointments. Then they drove to the cheaper apartment. The landlord was waiting. He showed them the apartment. Shinya and Peter were shocked. The apartment was very dirty. It smelled bad. The landlord tried to open a window, but it was stuck. In the kitchen, they saw a cockroach run across the floor.

2   "Don't worry," said the landlord. "It just needs a good cleaning. The last tenant who lived here wasn't very clean. And I'll fix the window."

3   When they looked at the bathroom, they found the faucet was leaking. Water was dripping into the sink.

continued

4   "Don't worry," said the landlord. "I'll fix that in no time. Let me show you the parking."

5   They went down thirty-five stairs (Peter counted) to get to the parking. It was very dark in the underground garage. Some of the lights weren't working. Two young men were standing in the corner of the garage. When they saw the landlord, Peter, and Shinya, they quickly hurried away. The landlord shouted something after them.

6   "Don't worry," he said to Shinya and Peter. "They don't live here. I'll get rid of them."

7   Shinya and Peter thanked the landlord and told him they would call him. Then they got Peter's car and drove off. "Well," said Shinya. "Climbing those stairs every day would be good exercise." They both started laughing.

8   The second apartment was easy to find. It was on a busy street near lots of shops. They went to the manager's office. This time the manager was a woman. First she showed Shinya and Peter the exercise room, indoor pool, and tanning spa. "Wow," said Peter. Shinya was watching a group of young people playing in the pool. "I like this apartment already," said Shinya.

9   Next the manager showed them around the apartment. It was very clean. Both bedrooms were a little small, but the living room was very large. There were lots of windows, and the apartment looked bright and sunny. There was an eating space in the kitchen, which opened up to a small but private patio.

10   "You need to let me know by this afternoon," said the manager. "I have lots of people who want to rent this apartment."

11   Peter and Shinya looked at each other. They nodded.

12   "We'll take it!" they said.

13   "Great," said the manager. You need to sign the lease for one year. I will need the first and last month's rent and a deposit of $500. I will return the $500 to you when

continued

you leave the apartment—if you don't break or damage anything. We will take care of cleaning the carpets and drapes. I also need the name of the person you are living with right now. I will call that person and ask for a reference. I want to know if you've ever gotten behind on your rent."

14   "No problem," said Shinya, watching the group of people having fun in the pool. "When can we move in?"

After You Read

Discussing the Reading

Work with a partner. Talk about the questions.

1. Do you think Shinya and Peter will be happy in the second apartment? Why or why not?

2. Would you like to live in either of these apartments? Why or why not?

3. In the final paragraph, Shinya is not really paying attention to the details about the lease. Is this a good idea? Explain your answer.

Check Your Understanding

A. Find and underline these words in Reading 2, Part B. Guess the meaning by looking at the context. Match the words with the correct definitions.

Word	Definition
__g__ 1. reference	a. a person who owns a house or apartment and rents it to someone
_____ 2. in no time	b. repair
_____ 3. landlord	c. surprised in a bad way
_____ 4. fix	d. money you pay that you will get back later
_____ 5. tenant	e. very quickly
_____ 6. shocked	f. a person who rents a house or apartment
_____ 7. deposit	g. information you give about someone you know very well to show they are a good worker or renter
_____ 8. leaking	h. when water is slowly coming out of something

B. Circle the letter of the best answer.

1. Which of these statements explains why Peter and Shinya were shocked at the first apartment?

   a. The rent was $600 a month.
   b. The landlord promised to fix everything.
   c. The apartment was in bad condition.

2. What was the only positive, or good, thing about the first apartment?

   a. The landlord was good at fixing things.
   b. Climbing the stairs to the garage was good exercise.
   c. The garage parking was very safe.

3. Why did Shinya like the second apartment before he even saw it?

   a. He liked the pool and the people swimming there.
   b. It was on a busy street.
   c. The manager was very helpful and friendly.

4. What was the only negative, or bad, thing about the second apartment?

   a. The rent was too expensive.
   b. The bedrooms were not very big.
   c. There was a private patio.

5. Why does Shinya say "No problem" in the last paragraph?

   a. He is thinking carefully about the reference, lease, rent, and deposit.
   b. He is reading the lease carefully and he agrees with the rules.
   c. He is watching the other tenants playing in the pool and is not paying attention to the manager.

6. Which statement is possible according to the reading?

   a. Shinya and Peter stay in the apartment for six months and then leave. They get the full deposit back because they kept the apartment in good condition.
   b. Shinya and Peter stay in the apartment for eighteen months and then leave. The microwave is broken. They get the full deposit back.
   c. Shinya and Peter stay in the apartment for two years. When they leave, the apartment is in good condition. They get the full deposit back.

The Homeless in America

Before You Read

Previewing

Do not read the complete article. Read the title and the headings. Look at the photo on page 67. Answer the questions. When you finish, share your answers in a group.

1. What do you think this reading is about?

    I think this reading _____.

2. What four questions does the writer ask?

    a. _____

    b. _____

    c. _____

    d. _____

3. Answer the questions without looking at the paragraphs in the reading. Talk about your answers in your group.

    a. _____

    b. _____

    c. _____

    d. _____

Previewing Vocabulary

These words are in Reading 3. Read the words and their definitions. Then choose the best word or words to complete each sentence.

Word	Definition
alcohol	a drink such as beer, wine, or vodka
mental illness	an illness of the mind
public place	a place like a park or a bus station where anyone can go
shelter	a building where homeless people can stay for a short time

1. The homeless family went to the _____, but it was full. They slept under a bridge that night.

2. "Would you like a beer?"

   "No thanks, I don't drink _____. I'll have a fruit juice, please."

3. When it is cold and wet, homeless people often go to a _____ such as a train station or library to keep warm and dry.

4. A _____ is a health problem just like a physical illness is. People need to see the doctor for medicine.

Now Read

The Homeless in America

Who Are the Homeless?

1   We have many incorrect ideas about homeless people. We think homeless people only live on the streets in big cities. In fact, they also live in shelters, in motels, in cars, in empty buildings, and in parks or other public places all over America. We think homeless people are usually single men. Not true: Mothers and children make up the largest group of homeless people. We also think people are homeless because they have drug, alcohol, or mental illnesses. Again, not correct. Most people are homeless because they are poor.

How Many People Are Homeless in the U.S.?

2   About 3.5 million people are homeless for some period of time every year in America. Over a third of these people are children. However, it is difficult to say

continued

exactly how many people are homeless in the United States. When organizations try to count the number of homeless people, they often count the number of people who are living in shelters. However, there are not enough shelters for homeless people. Shelters turn away 37% of people who need a bed for the night. So the number of homeless people is much higher than the number of people living in shelters. It is also difficult to give accurate numbers because many homeless people hide. They move around from one place to another, and they sleep in empty buildings or cars. So no one knows exactly how many people are homeless in the United States.

Why Are People Homeless?

3   Most people are homeless because they are poor. In 2000, 11.3% of the U.S. population (31.1 million people) was poor. Many people today cannot find work. They are unemployed. Others have jobs but cannot earn enough money to pay for rent and child care. In the last few years, rents have increased, or gone up, faster than wages. In addition to rent, families often have to pay over $1,000 a month for full-time child care for two children.

4   There are other reasons why people become homeless. Some people become very sick, but have no health insurance. In 2000, 38.7 million Americans had no health insurance. Some of these people lose their jobs because they are sick and have expensive doctor's bills. They can't pay hospital bills, and they get behind on

continued

their rent. Their landlord evicts them, and they become homeless. Another reason is domestic violence. Domestic violence is when one person in a family is violent to, or hurts, another family member. Usually, women and children are the victims of domestic violence. Almost half of all homeless women and children are escaping from domestic violence. A third reason for being homeless is mental illness and drug or alcohol problems. When people are poor and suffer from these problems, it is very difficult to get medical help, but it is very easy to end up living on the streets.

What Is the Answer?

5   There is no easy answer to this problem. We need more cheap housing. We need more jobs, higher wages, and job training. We need to help people who have serious problems that affect their lives. Most of all, we need to understand the problem before we can find the answers.

After You Read

How Well Did You Read?

Read the statements. Write *T* (true) or *F* (false).

_____ 1. Many people have false ideas about homeless people.

_____ 2. There are enough shelters for homeless people in America.

_____ 3. Mental illness is the main reason why people are homeless.

_____ 4. There is no simple answer to the problem of homeless people.

Discussing the Reading

Work with a partner. Talk about the questions.

1. Why are people homeless according to this article? Can you think of any other reasons why people can become homeless?

2. What is domestic violence? According to this article, many women and children run away from a violent boyfriend or husband. Why do you think they run away? Why don't they call the police?

3. Are you surprised that there are so many homeless people in America? Why or why not?

Check Your Understanding

Circle the letter of the best answer.

1. Which statement is correct according to the reading?

    a. About 3,000,500 people are homeless in America.
    b. About 1,170,000 homeless people are children.
    c. More than a third of homeless people live in shelters.

2. Why is it difficult to find out exactly how many people are homeless?

    a. because not all homeless people live in shelters, and they are difficult to find
    b. because homeless people are poor and have no health insurance
    c. because some homeless people sleep in their cars

3. *When organizations try to count the number of homeless people, **they** often count the number of people who are living in shelters.*

    They refers to

    a. organizations.
    b. homeless people.
    c. the number of people who are living in shelters.

4. *Many people today cannot find work. They are **unemployed**. Others have jobs but cannot earn enough money to pay for rent and child care.*

    Unemployed means

    a. working.
    b. not working.
    c. looking for work.

5. Which statement is correct according to the reading?

    a. Most people become homeless because they cannot buy health insurance.
    b. Most people are homeless because they do not have enough money to pay for things like rent, health insurance, and child care.
    c. Wages have increased faster than rents in the last few years.

6. *In 2000, 38.7 million Americans had no health insurance. Some of these people lose their jobs because they are sick and have expensive doctor's bills. They can't pay hospital bills, and they get behind on the rent. Their landlord **evicts** them, and they become homeless.*

    Evict means

    a. tell someone they must pay rent on time.
    b. call the police.
    c. force someone to leave their rented house or apartment.

continued

7. Read this sentence from the last paragraph.

*There is no easy answer to **this** problem.*

This refers to

   a. mental illness and drug/alcohol problems.
   b. domestic violence.
   c. being homeless.

8. Why is there no easy answer to this problem?

   a. because homeless people have a lot of problems
   b. because there are different reasons why people become homeless
   c. both of the above

Vocabulary Review

A. Choose the best word or words to complete each sentence.

landlord	maximum	leaking	deposit
get over	detests	advantages	evicted
punctual	utility bills		

1. I was very sick last month with the flu. It took me two weeks to
   _____ it.

2. Paul likes tea, but he _____ coffee. He says even the smell
   of coffee makes him sick.

3. The apartment was a mess. It was very dirty, and water was
   _____ from the refrigerator.

4. There are several _____ to living with a host family. You
   don't have to cook, you can improve your English, and you can make friends
   with Americans.

5. Lee found an advertisement for an apartment. He called the
   _____ and asked if he could come and see the apartment.

6. In the winter, _____ are higher than in the summer. We use
   more electricity or gas to heat a house in the winter.

7. Suzi and Lee looked after the apartment very well. When they left, the landlord
   gave them back their _____ of $500.

8. Most British people are very _____. They do not like to be late.

9. The landlord _____ my neighbors because they didn't pay the rent.

10. The _____ number of people allowed on the bus is 24. If there are 24 people on the bus, you have to wait for the next bus.

B. Complete the sentences using your own words.

1. My friend and I are very good tenants because we _____.

2. It is dangerous to drink alcohol _____.

3. The woman took her children to a shelter because _____.

4. In American culture, it is rude to _____.

5. I find it difficult to get down to _____.

6. Alex missed class because _____.

7. Many people can't afford _____.

8. He was unemployed for a long time because _____.

9. The teacher said, "Don't get behind on your _____."

10. My landlord needs to fix _____.

Expanding the Topic

Connecting Reading with Writing

A. Choose one of the following questions and answer it in complete sentences. Use information and vocabulary you have learned from the chapter.

1. Would you like to stay with a host family? Why or why not?

2. What are the advantages to living in an apartment?

3. What are the disadvantages to living in an apartment?

B. Are there many homeless people in the country or city where you were born? Write a paragraph that answers this question. Explain why there are or are not a lot of homeless people there.

C. Look at this illustration. Imagine you are this homeless person. How do you feel? What are you thinking? Write a paragraph that explains what it is like to be this homeless person. Begin like this:

It is another very cold day. I am sitting

_____

_____

_____

_____

_____

_____

Exploring Online

Choose one of the following assignments. Use the Internet to find information.

1. You and a friend want to move to a new apartment. You need two bedrooms and two bathrooms. The apartment must be near your school. Go online. Choose a major search engine. Type in *apartments* + the name of your school. Print the advertisement and bring it to class.

2. You have a friend who is an international student. She wants to find a host family. She asks you to help because she does not have a computer. Go online. Type in *host families* + the name of your city. Find a host family organization in your area. Then complete the following letter to your friend:

Dear Pham,

I found a host family organization. It is called _____ _____. Their telephone number is _____.
You can e-mail them at this address: _____. This organization says that they have lots of good host families. It costs _____ a month. I hope this helps. I'm looking forward to seeing you again!

Best regards,

_____

CHAPTER

4

Reaching Out Across the World

This chapter is about international aid organizations that help people in times of trouble. In Reading 1, you will learn about an organization that helps people who do not have very much money build new homes. Reading 2 is about two of the biggest international aid organizations—the Red Cross and the Red Crescent. Reading 3 is about search-and-rescue teams that help when there is a serious earthquake.

In this chapter, you will practice:

Reading Skills

➡ Previewing a reading

➡ Understanding general versus specific ideas

➡ Finding paragraph topics

Vocabulary Skills

➡ Using context clues to understand vocabulary

➡ Previewing vocabulary

➡ Understanding phrasal verbs with *break*

Life Skills

➡ Completing more advanced Internet searches

Before You Read

Previewing

Discuss the questions with a partner.

1. Read the title of Reading 1. What does it mean?
2. Look at the photo on page 78. What are these people doing?

<table>
<tr><td>

Reading Skill

</td><td>

Understanding General Versus Specific Ideas

In this chapter, you will practice finding paragraph topics. A paragraph has one general topic and several specific ideas. Before you practice finding a topic, you must understand the difference between a general topic and a specific idea.

A *general* topic is a word or phrase that includes several details.

A *specific* idea is just one detail or example.

    Example:

    General topic: grammar

    Specific ideas: verbs, nouns, adjectives

</td></tr>
</table>

A. Read these groups of words. Underline the general word or phrase in each group. The first one is done for you.

1. international students, students of English, resident students, <u>students</u>
2. Spain, Europe, Germany, France, Great Britain
3. small, huge, size, large, big
4. rock, pop, music, classical, jazz
5. beautiful, unusual, red, old, adjective
6. science, biology, physics, chemistry, geology
7. cat, pet, dog, bird, snake
8. French, German, Spanish, language, Japanese

continued

9. SUVs, trucks, vehicles, cars, convertibles

10. brother, mother, aunt, cousin, relative

B. Read these general words. Add three specific words to each general word.

1. Africa   _____Nigeria_____   _____   _____

2. schools   _____   _____   _____

3. meals   _____   _____   _____

4. singers   _____   _____   _____

5. difficult jobs   _____   _____   _____

Using Context Clues to Understand Vocabulary

The words in bold print are in Reading 1. Guess the meaning of each word by looking at the context. Circle the letter of the best answer.

1. When we bought our house, we borrowed money from the bank. Every month we pay this money back to the bank by paying the **mortgage**.

   a. money you have in the bank
   b. money you pay toward the cost of your home
   c. money you are saving each month

2. Ten years ago, I bought my house for $150,000. I sold it for $200,000. I made a **profit** of $50,000.

   a. money you must pay back to someone
   b. money you make from selling something at a higher cost than you bought it for
   c. money you save in the bank

3. All people should have **affordable** health insurance. If health insurance does not cost very much, everyone will have insurance.

   a. that you can buy because you have enough money
   b. that you cannot buy because it is too expensive
   c. that you dream about buying

4. I borrowed $500 from my parents to buy a car. They told me I had to pay 10% **interest** on the money. When I paid them back, I paid them $550.

   a. something you like doing
   b. money you must pay for borrowing money
   c. ten percent of a number

5. **Low-income** families do not earn enough money for important things like rent and child care.

   a. homeless
   b. with young children
   c. not having very much money

Now Read

Building a Home, Building a Life

1   Habitat for Humanity is an international organization. It helps low-income people build their own homes. Two Americans, Millard and Linda Fuller, started this organization in the 1970s. They believed that all people should have a safe, affordable home. The Fullers' goal was to build thousands of inexpensive houses for families who could not afford their own homes. So they started Habitat for Humanity.

2   Habitat for Humanity works in this way. People from all over the world donate, or give, money to this organization. The Habitat organizers use this money to build a house. Many volunteers help with the building. Because the organization does not pay the volunteers, it does not cost very much to build the house. The new homeowner must also help build. When the house is finished, the Habitat homeowner pays the money back to Habitat each month. This is called a mortgage. However, Habitat makes no profit from the house and charges no interest. So, because the house didn't cost very much, the homeowner can afford to pay the mortgage each month. This money goes back into the Habitat fund. Organizers can then use it to build another new house.

3   People all over the world have better lives today because of Habitat for Humanity. This organization has built more than 150,000 houses for families in 89 countries including America, Great Britain, Mexico, India, Russia, South Africa, and Haiti. The houses are simple, but safe and warm. Habitat homeowners say that they have better lives when they have their own home. It is easier to keep a job, stay healthy, and send children to school if you live in a safe home. The whole family benefits from the Habitat house.

4   Habitat for Humanity usually builds more than one home at a time in a community. There are several reasons for doing this. First, it is easier, quicker, and cheaper for volunteers to build a number of houses at the same time and in the same place. There are also advantages for the community. While the homeowners are building their homes together, they get to know each other. They become good

continued

friends and they learn new skills. When one house is finished, a Habitat homeowner helps build a neighbor's house. Working together helps build a strong community. When all the houses are finished, the homeowners feel proud of their community and want to look after it.

5   Volunteers are an extremely important part of Habitat for Humanity. Yet building a house is hard work. Who would want to volunteer to do a difficult job and not get any money for the work? People volunteer for many reasons. All volunteers want to help people. They all believe everyone should live in a good home. Many volunteers have had a good life, and they want to give back to others who are not so fortunate. Some people volunteer because they want to meet other people. Others volunteer because they are trying to get some work experience. These volunteers are the heart of this organization.

6   People all over the world dream of owning their own home. Habitat for Humanity has helped thousands of families live this dream. In the future, it will help new families build homes and build a better life.

After You Read

How Well Did You Read?

Read the statements. Write *T* (true), *F* (false), or *N* (not enough information).

_____ 1. Habitat for Humanity builds houses only for low-income families.

_____ 2. Habitat homeowners help to build their houses.

_____ 3. Habitat houses cost more than other houses.

_____ 4. Habitat homeowners always pay their mortgages on time.

Discussing the Reading

Work in small groups. Talk about the questions.

1. Why are Habitat houses cheaper than other houses?

2. Habitat houses are "simple, but safe and warm." What do you think this means?

3. According to this reading, homeowners learn new skills while they are building their houses. What kinds of skills do they learn? How will these skills help them in the future?

4. Why do people volunteer, according to this reading? Can you think of other reasons why people volunteer?

5. Have you ever been a volunteer? What work did you do? Why did you volunteer?

Check Your Understanding

Circle the letter of the best answer.

1. The Fullers believed _____.

   a. they could build expensive houses for low-income people
   b. low-income people didn't need help
   c. everyone should be able to buy a house

2. Habitat houses are inexpensive to build partly because _____.

   a. the materials are cheap
   b. Habitat pays low wages to its workers
   c. Habitat workers are not paid wages

3. Habitat homeowners can pay the mortgage because _____.

   a. they have good jobs
   b. the monthly payments are low
   c. the neighbors help them

continued

4. According to this reading, it is cheaper to build _____.

    a. one house in each community
    b. a few houses in each community
    c. houses overseas in countries such as Mexico and India

5. *The whole family **benefits** from the Habitat house.*

    Benefits means _____.

    a. pays for something
    b. is helped by something
    c. builds together

6. *The Fullers' **goal** was to build thousands of inexpensive houses for families who could not afford their own homes.*

    Goal means _____.

    a. answer
    b. dream
    c. problem

7. Why do you think work experience is important for some volunteers?

    a. They are looking for a job, and they need more experience.
    b. They enjoy working with their hands.
    c. They need more experience in building.

8. Which statement is correct according to the reading?

    a. The Fullers reached their goal and stopped building low-income houses.
    b. The Fullers are still trying to reach their goal.
    c. The Fullers reached their goal, but they are still building low-income houses.

Finding Paragraph Topics

A **paragraph** is a group of sentences about a general topic. You need to identify this topic in order to understand the whole paragraph. To find the **topic,** you need to ask, "Who (or what) is this paragraph about?" The answer to this question is the paragraph topic. The paragraph topic should not be too general or too specific.

Example:

There are several reasons why it is a good idea to volunteer while you are a student. First, you can learn a lot as a volunteer. You can learn to work with other people, and you can gain new skills. Next, you can also meet and make new friends. Finally, volunteering will help you when you apply for a new job. So, if you have some free time, think about becoming a volunteer. You won't be sorry.

What is this paragraph about?

a. volunteers
b. learning a lot as a volunteer
c. reasons why it is a good idea to volunteer

Answer a: This answer is too general. The paragraph does talk about volunteers, but the topic needs to give more information about what the paragraph says about volunteers.
Answer b: This answer is too specific. It gives just one detail in the paragraph.
Answer c: This answer is correct. It is not too general, and it is not too specific. It tells us the general subject of the paragraph.

A. **Work with a partner. Read the paragraphs. Circle the letter of the topic of each paragraph.**

1. People can volunteer in many different ways. Parents can go to their children's schools and help in the classroom, in the office, or on the playground. You can volunteer in a hospital. Many people enjoy meeting patients in a hospital and helping the patients feel better. If you love animals, you can always volunteer at a pet shelter or at a zoo. If you want to volunteer, you will find there are many different opportunities.

   Topic:
   a. volunteers at schools
   b. volunteering
   c. different ways to volunteer

continued

2. Thousands of people need affordable, safe houses. However, buying a home is not easy for low-income families. Houses are too expensive. Even if both parents are working, they often do not have enough money to buy a house. It is even more difficult if the family has young children because child care is so expensive.

Topic:
a. affordable, safe houses
b. problems with buying a house
c. the cost of child care

3. Many students rent houses or apartments while they are in college. Before they rent, they should do the following things. Check the apartment very carefully. Does everything work okay? Talk to the manager. Ask about the rent. How much is it? When do you pay it? Ask about the deposit. How much is it? Finally, read the lease very carefully.

Topic:
a. renting
b. ask about the rent
c. things to do before you rent

B. **Work with a partner. These questions are about paragraphs from Reading 1. Circle the letter of the best answer.**

1. Read paragraph 2 again. What is the topic of this paragraph?

   a. how Habitat for Humanity works
   b. building houses
   c. paying the mortgage

2. Read paragraph 3 again. What is the topic of this paragraph?

   a. building better lives
   b. advantages of owning a home
   c. building houses in many countries

3. Read paragraph 4 again. What is the topic of this paragraph?

   a. building a home
   b. advantages of building several houses at the same place and at the same time
   c. helping a community

4. Read paragraph 5 again. What is the topic of this paragraph?

   a. volunteers
   b. the importance of volunteers
   c. why people volunteer

The Red Cross and the Red Crescent

Before You Read

Previewing

Discuss the questions with a partner.

1. The two flags are the flags for the Red Cross and the Red Crescent. Do you know why one flag has a cross and the other flag has a crescent?

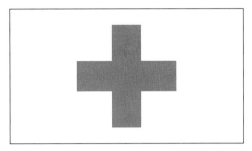 

2. The Red Cross and the Red Crescent help people who are in trouble. How do they help people? Write down three things you know about these organizations.

   a. _____

   b. _____

   c. _____

Previewing Vocabulary

These words are in Reading 2. Read the words and their definitions. Then choose the best word to complete each sentence.

Word	Definition
swords	weapons with long sharp blades, used in past times
wounded	injured, hurt
begging	asking for something in an anxious way because you need it very much
shocked	feeling very upset by something unexpected and bad
symbol	a shape or a picture that has a special meaning
hurricane	a very strong and dangerous storm
bullets	small pieces of metal you shoot from a gun

1. In 2003, a _____ hit South Carolina. The strong winds knocked out power for millions of homes.

continued

2. I saw an elderly woman _____ for food. She had a sign that said "Please help me."

3. Atsuko was _____ when she saw homeless people in the U.S. She thought everyone was rich in that country.

4. The _____ soldier hid in a shelter until the fighting stopped. Then he waited for his friends to come and help him.

5. A red cross on a white background is the _____ of the Red Cross.

6. Many years ago, soldiers used _____, not guns, when they fought. These weapons were made of metal and were very sharp.

7. New guns can fire many _____ in just seconds. These guns are very dangerous.

Now Read

The Red Cross and the Red Crescent

1   Bullets screamed by, swords clashed. Rain pounded down and thunder rocked the skies. Two hundred thousand soldiers on the battlefield; two hundred thousand men trying to kill each other. The noise was deafening. Everywhere there were shouts of anger, fear, and pain. And when the rain finally stopped, and the smoke cleared, forty thousand wounded men lay in the grass. There were no ambulances, no doctors, no nurses. Just thousands of men from three different armies begging for help in three different languages.

2   The year was 1859; the place, Solferino in Northern Italy. A Swiss businessman called Henri Durant was near the village of Solferino when this terrible battle happened. He was shocked at the number of people killed. He was even more shocked that there was nobody to help the wounded soldiers. He knew many of these soldiers would die if they didn't get medical help. So he organized the people of Solferino. He asked them to help the wounded soldiers. At first, the Italian villagers refused to help the soldiers who were not Italian. They only wanted to help their own soldiers. They did not want to help the other armies. "No," said Durant, "*Tutti fratelli*—they are all brothers." So the people of Solferino helped all the soldiers.

3   Durant could not forget the Battle of Solferino. He knew there would be more wars in the future. He believed volunteers should help these soldiers. Back in Switzerland, he wrote a book about this idea. He also talked to other businessmen. A

continued

lot of people agreed with him. In 1863, people from sixteen countries met in Geneva. They started the Red Cross. The countries agreed that this organization would help all people in times of war. When the Franco-Prussian War broke out in 1870, British and Dutch Red Cross volunteers were ready to help soldiers on both sides.

4   The twentieth century was a busy one hundred years for the Red Cross. During this time, the Red Cross grew to become the largest international aid organization in the world. Red Cross organizations started in many different countries. In Muslim countries such as Iran, Iraq, and Pakistan, the organization was called the Red Crescent because a cross is a symbol of the Christian religion. The Red Cross and the Red Crescent helped people in many terrible wars, including the two world wars. In addition, volunteers helped millions of people who suffered from natural disasters, such as earthquakes and hurricanes. When AIDS was discovered at the end of the century, the Red Cross and the Red Crescent worked to educate people about this terrible disease.

5   The twenty-first century has brought new wars and problems. The Red Cross was there to help during the September 11 attacks in America. The Red Crescent has also helped victims of the wars in Afghanistan and Iraq that followed the 9/11 attacks. International organizations from all over the world rushed to Iran in the early weeks of 2004 when a huge earthquake hit Bam and killed over forty thousand people. Meanwhile, organizations continue to help the millions of people who suffer from AIDS.

6   Henri Durant believed that people are all brothers. The Red Cross and the Red Crescent have been very successful because they continue to believe this. They do not take sides in a war; they help everyone. As the world continues to be a difficult and dangerous place for millions of people, the Red Cross and the Red Crescent will be there to help.

After You Read

How Well Did You Read?

Read the statements. Write *T* (true), *F* (false), or *N* (not enough information).

_____ 1. Men from all three armies were wounded in the battle of Solferino.

_____ 2. Henri Durant was fighting for the Swiss army.

_____ 3. More soldiers died in the Battle of Solferino than in any other battle.

_____ 4. In a war, the Red Cross and the Red Crescent only help one army.

Discussing the Reading

Work with a partner. Talk about the questions.

1. What do you think Durant meant when he said "They are all brothers"?

2. What did the villagers first say when Durant asked them to help the wounded soldiers? Do you think they were right or wrong to say this?

3. Why do you think the article says the world continues to be a "difficult and dangerous place for millions of people"? Can you give examples of difficult and dangerous places to live?

Check Your Understanding

Circle the letter of the best answer.

1. In this reading, the first paragraph _____.

   a. explains why the Red Cross began
   b. gives information about the man who started the Red Cross
   c. describes a famous battle in history

2. In Solferino, the villagers did not want to help all the wounded soldiers because _____.

   a. They didn't want to help soldiers from different countries
   b. there were too many wounded soldiers
   c. the villagers did not know how to help the wounded soldiers

3. Why did the villagers decide to help all the soldiers?

   a. They agreed with Henri Durant.
   b. They were afraid of the soldiers.
   c. They liked the soldiers.

4. People decided to start the Red Cross because _____.

   a. they wanted to stop future wars
   b. they wanted to help soldiers in future wars
   c. they wanted to help volunteers in future wars

5. *The twentieth* **century** *was a busy one hundred years for the Red Cross.* **Century** means _____.

   a. twenty years
   b. many years
   c. one hundred years

6. Which statement is correct?

   a. Muslim countries have the same name and symbol as the Red Cross.
   b. Muslim countries have a different name and different symbol than the Red Cross.
   c. Muslim countries have the same symbol as the Red Cross but a different name.

7. Reread paragraph 4. What is the topic of this paragraph?

    a. the Red Cross and the Red Crescent
    b. the Red Cross and the Red Crescent in the twentieth century
    c. Red Cross volunteers

8. *In addition, volunteers helped millions of people who suffered from* **natural disasters** *such as earthquakes and hurricanes.*
Natural disasters are _____.

    a. dangerous things that happen because of nature
    b. terrible things that happen because of people
    c. bad things that happen in times of war

9. Reread paragraph 5. Which problem or war began in the twentieth century and is still continuing today?

    a. AIDS
    b. the September 11 attack on America
    c. the Bam earthquake in Iran

10. The Red Cross and the Red Crescent have been very successful because _____.

    a. Henri Durant started these organizations to help people in times of war
    b. people will always need help
    c. the organizations don't choose who is right or wrong—they help everyone

---

Vocabulary Skill

Understanding Phrasal Verbs with Break

Reread this sentence from Reading 2: *When the Franco-Prussian War* **broke out** *in 1870, British and Dutch Red Cross volunteers were ready to help soldiers on both sides.* **Break out** means that something bad like a fire or a war begins. Here are some more phrasal verbs using *break:*

break down	stop working because something is broken
break into	enter a building using force in order to steal something
break off	break a piece from the main part of something
break through	force a way through something
break up	end a romantic relationship or a marriage

Choose the best phrasal verb from the list on page 87 to complete each sentence. Use the past tense.

1. When our lawn mower _____, my father asked me to fix it.

2. People were not surprised when the movie star _____ with her husband. It was, after all, her fourth marriage.

3. After a gray, rainy day, the sun finally _____ the clouds.

4. Last week someone _____ my car, but luckily the alarm started and the person ran away before getting anything.

5. I need to go to the dentist. Part of my tooth _____ yesterday and it hurts.

Reading 3 *Earthquake! A Survivor's Tale*

Before You Read

Previewing

Discuss the questions with a partner.

1. What is the general topic of this reading?

2. Look at the photos on pages 89 and 91. Describe the photos in a general way.

3. Look at the photos again. Talk about a specific detail from each photo.

Using Context Clues to Understand Vocabulary

The words in bold print are in Reading 3. Guess the meaning of each word by looking at the context. Circle the letter of the best answer.

1. There was a fire in the house next to mine. The family was sleeping at the time. Luckily, firefighters **rescued** everyone, and no one was hurt.

   a. saved
   b. called
   c. saw

2. It was snowing, and the wind was blowing hard. I was so cold, my hands were **shaking.** I couldn't keep them still.

   a. freezing
   b. moving quickly
   c. hurting

3. In 1990, there was a bad earthquake in San Francisco. A freeway **collapsed.** It landed on cars and trucks.

   a. burned
   b. suddenly fell down
   c. shook

4. Last night there was a terrible storm. A **huge** tree fell on my neighbor's house. It covered the whole house.

   a. small
   b. medium sized
   c. very large

5. It was a long movie. It **lasted** almost three hours.

   a. continued for a period of time
   b. started
   c. finished

Now Read

Earthquake! A Survivor's Tale

1   On August 17, 1999, a huge earthquake hit Turkey. It happened at night, while most people were sleeping. The earthquake was 7.8 on the Richter Scale. It only lasted forty-five seconds, but it caused a lot of damage, especially in Izmit. This was

continued

the center of the earthquake. Hundreds of buildings collapsed. When the buildings fell down, many people were under them. Sadly, thousands of people died.

2 Volunteers from Turkey and many other countries quickly came to help. Some countries sent search-and-rescue teams that arrived a few hours after the quake happened. These teams have dogs that can find people trapped under buildings. When the dogs find someone alive, they bark. The rescue teams hear the dog. They then know someone is under the building. They try to save the person. In this story, a search-and-rescue team from Germany worked with local Turkish volunteers. They found a woman who was trapped under a building for many hours. This is the woman's story:

3 I was asleep when it happened—when the earth moved and my world changed. The first thing I remember is hearing a tinkle of metal shaking against glass. This was my earthquake alarm. I always sleep with a glass of water next to me. In the glass, I put a teaspoon. My son told me I would hear the spoon shaking against the glass if there was an earthquake. Well, I heard it, but it didn't help me. Everything happened too fast. I couldn't get out. No one could.

4 I heard a terrible noise. It sounded like a train breaking through my apartment. My bed began to shake. It shook so badly I couldn't get up. I fell back onto the bed. I put the covers over my head and said a prayer. Everywhere around me, things were crashing. Then the earth moved. I fell off my bed. The world turned dark, and it became very quiet.

5 I don't know how long I was unconscious. When I woke up, I opened my eyes; I couldn't believe I was alive. I was lying on my back looking straight up. There was wood and metal and parts of the ceiling over me. There was dust everywhere. Thick, white dust. It was difficult to breathe. I couldn't move. Something was on my legs and one arm was trapped under me. It was very quiet and very dark. I could hear water dripping somewhere above me. I didn't know if it was day or night. I lay there and thought of my son. I knew he was looking for me. I knew he would search until he found me. I just had to wait.

6 Time passed slowly. It was hot, and the air smelled bad. Sometimes I didn't know if I was awake or dreaming. My mouth was dry. Water was dripping on to my leg, but I couldn't reach it.

continued

7   After a long time, I suddenly heard someone shouting. It was my son! "Can you hear me?" he called. I tried to call back, but I couldn't talk. The dust had taken my voice. I was too frightened to move because I thought everything would crash down on me. So I lay silently, and the voice moved away.

8   I was dreaming about a summer picnic. My son and his family were there. We were by the water. A dog was running through the water and barking. It sounded happy. Then I realized I really could hear a dog. I was awake. A dog was barking above me. The dog barked again. It didn't go away. It was the most wonderful sound in the world.

9   Several hours later, volunteer rescuers from the United States, Germany, and Turkey lifted this woman to safety. She was weak and dehydrated because she was without water for nineteen hours, and she had a broken leg. As they lifted her from the collapsed apartment building, a large German shepherd dog barked happily at her side. Her son told her the dog saved her life. He told her they couldn't find anyone in the building until the dog helped them. The woman smiled at the dog, and the dog licked her tired, dust-covered face.

After You Read

How Well Did You Read?

Read the sentences. Write *T* (true), *F* (false), or *N* (not enough information).

_____ 1. The woman was trapped under the building for two days.

_____ 2. The woman's son found her.

_____ 3. Her son thought he would never find his mother.

_____ 4. Volunteers from several countries helped Turkey after the earthquake.

Check Your Understanding

A. Circle the letter of the best answer.

1. The August 1999 earthquake caused a huge amount of damage because _____.

   a. it lasted for a long time
   b. it was a very strong earthquake
   c. it happened at night

2. A few hours after the quake happened, _____.

   a. the search-and-rescue team found the woman
   b. international volunteers came to help
   c. buildings collapsed

3. The first thing the woman heard was _____.

   a. a loud noise like a train
   b. the sound of things crashing around her
   c. the teaspoon shaking against the glass of water

4. The woman thought she would be rescued because _____.

   a. she could hear water dripping
   b. she knew her son would look for her
   c. she knew international volunteers were looking for her

5. *I don't know how long I was **unconscious**. When I woke up, I opened my eyes; I couldn't believe I was alive.*

   Unconscious means _____.

   a. not awake
   b. lying down
   c. dreaming

6. The son moved away from where his mother was trapped because _____.

   a. he couldn't hear anything
   b. it was dangerous
   c. he gave up looking for his mother

7. When the woman heard the dog, _____.

   a. she was with her son on a picnic
   b. she thought she was dreaming
   c. she called out for help

8. *The dog barked again. It didn't go away. **It** was the most wonderful sound in the world.*

   It refers to _____.

   a. the sound of the dog barking
   b. the world
   c. the volunteers

9. *She was weak and **dehydrated** because she was without water for nineteen hours, and she had a broken leg.*

   Dehydrated means _____.

   a. sick from having no food
   b. sick from not drinking enough
   c. sick from having a broken leg

10. This was an international rescue because _____.

    a. a German Shepherd dog found her
    b. search-and-rescue teams from several countries saved her
    c. it happened in Turkey

B. The search-and-rescue team completed this report about the rescue. Read the report carefully.

August 18, 1999

Search-and-Rescue Team #4 Members:
Gert Becker (leader)
Jan Frieman
Herman Klaus & Beno (dog)

Mission: Earthquake Search and Rescue, Izmit, Turkey

Team notes:

1   We arrived in Istanbul just before noon on the 17th. Red Crescent trucks took us to the city of Izmit, which is about 55 miles southeast of the capital. This was the center of the earthquake. In many parts of the city, most of the buildings had collapsed. People were digging with their hands trying to find anyone who was alive.

2   Our team went to a building that was not damaged. Turkish volunteers welcomed us. We unloaded our gear and fed and watered Beno.

3   A local police officer told us about an apartment building. They searched the building at 9:00 that morning. It was very dangerous. When they tried to get inside, parts of the building collapsed. They heard nothing, but a man said his mother was inside the building. They asked us to send the dog in to check for survivors.

4   A guide took us to the building. It was badly damaged. Ten floors had collapsed like a pancake. As we watched, more bricks fell. We couldn't send people in—it was too dangerous.

5   Herman got Beno ready while the team found a good place for Beno to start the search. There was a small opening on the north side of the building. Herman pointed at it and told Beno to search. It was 3:00 p.m.—exactly 12 hours since the earthquake. The dog went off, and we stepped back and waited.

6   The dog returned after ten minutes. It had found no one alive. We moved to the south side and again sent Beno in. This time, we heard barking after only a few minutes. We got our climbing and cutting equipment ready. We radioed for more help. An American team and Turkish police officers joined us.

7   It took us four hours to find the woman and get her out. At 7:15 p.m., Red Crescent workers took her to a hospital, and team #4 returned to the base. The team slept five hours and then returned to the center to start our second rescue.

Teachers sometimes ask students to answer questions about a reading in complete sentences. If you make a serious grammar mistake in a sentence, the teacher may not be able to understand your answer. So, it is important to use accurate grammar as you write.

The question can help you find the subject of your answer and the correct verb and tense.

Examples:

1. Where *was* <u>the center of the earthquake?</u>

   <u>The center of the earthquake</u> *was* in Izmit.

2. How *did* <u>the search and rescue team</u> *find* <u>the trapped woman?</u>

   <u>The search and rescue team</u> *found* <u>the trapped woman</u> because the dog barked.

3. Why *did* <u>the dog</u> *bark*?

   <u>The dog</u> *barked* because it found the woman.

C. Use information from Reading 3 and the team report to answer these questions. Answer in complete sentences. Remember to use the question to help you write your answer.

1. What time did the earthquake happen?

   _____

2. Where was the search-and-rescue team from?

   _____

3. Who was the leader of the team?

   _____

4. Who searched the apartment building earlier in the day?

   _____

5. Why did the search-and-rescue team decide they couldn't send people to search for survivors?

   _____

6. Was the woman in the north or the south side of the building?

   _____

7. How did the woman know her rescuers were not Turkish?

   _____

8. What time was the woman rescued?

   _____

continued

9. Who took the woman to the hospital?

_____

10. What did the German team do when Red Crescent workers took the woman to the hospital?

_____

Understanding General Versus Specific Ideas

Look at the photo. Answer the question and then complete the task. When you finish, share your answers in a group.

1. What is the general topic of this photo?

_____

2. Write down three specific details you can see in the photo.

a. _____

b. _____

c. _____

Choosing the Correct Word Form

Choose the correct word forms to complete each sentence. When you use a verb, use the correct tense and make the verb agree with its subject. The numbers in the chart corresponds to the question numbers.

	Verb	Noun	Adjective
1.	agree	agreement	agreeable
2.	educate	education	educated
3.	believe	belief	believable
4.	decide	decision	decisive
5.	volunteer	volunteer	voluntary
6.	benefit	benefit	beneficial
7.	increase	increase	
8.	evict	eviction	

1. The landlord asked us to read and then sign the _____. He _____ to let us take it home to read it.

2. In this year's election, many people are saying that _____ is an important issue. People believe that schools need more money in order to _____ all children.

3. I couldn't _____ my eyes! The movie was so _____ I thought the dinosaurs were going to walk right out into the theatre.

4. The manager was very _____. He made his _____ quickly and then would not change his mind.

5. We need more _____ to help at the homeless shelter. I'm going to ask my mother to _____ tonight.

6. Last year I _____ from a tax cut. I paid less tax. I hope there will be another _____ this year.

7. The landlord _____ my rent last month. Because of this _____, I now need to look for a cheaper apartment.

8. My friends got behind in their rent—six months behind. A few days ago, their landlord _____ them. When I heard about the _____, I wasn't surprised.

Vocabulary Review

A. Choose the best word or words to complete each sentence.

century	symbol	shocked	goal
low-income	affordable	lasted	dehydrated
mortgage	survivors		

1. Everyone needs _____ health insurance. If you do not have enough money to pay for insurance, you are in trouble when you get sick and need a doctor.

2. The math test _____ two hours. When it was over, I felt very tired.

3. Miho was _____ when she saw several homeless people in downtown Chicago. She didn't think people were so poor in America.

4. My _____ for the future is to learn English so that I can take regular college-level courses. I will work hard to succeed in doing this.

5. The last _____ saw many wars, including two world wars. Hopefully, the next one hundred years will be more peaceful.

6. _____ students can apply for financial aid to help pay for the cost of college.

7. The Red Crescent uses a different _____ on its flag than the Red Cross. It has a crescent instead of a cross.

8. In hot weather, you need to drink lots of water. If you don't, you may become _____ and get very sick.

9. Last week a plane crashed. Ten people died, but luckily there were more than fifty _____. These people were able to get out of the plane quickly.

10. I rented a house for a long time. Then my wife and I bought our own house. The _____ payment is about the same as I paid in rent.

B. Complete the sentences using your own words.

1. Last year, my business didn't make a profit because _____.

2. The student was very lazy. She refused to _____.

3. I knew the child was unconscious because _____.

4. People volunteer because _____.

5. The President's plane took off at _____.

6. My hand was shaking because I _____.

7. Firefighters rescue _____.

8. The bridge across the river collapsed because _____.

9. People moved into the hurricane shelters when _____.

10. Examples of natural disasters are _____.

Expanding the Topic

Connecting Reading with Writing

Answer the questions in complete sentences. Use information and vocabulary you have learned in this chapter.

1. Why can many families not afford to buy their own house?

2. What are two reasons why people volunteer?

3. Why are the Red Cross and the Red Crescent such important organizations?

4. What happens when there is a bad earthquake?

5. Why do search-and-rescue teams sometimes use dogs to help rescue people?

Exploring Online

Completing More Advanced Internet Searches

The Web has millions of Web sites, so it is sometimes difficult to find the information you need. To search effectively, give the search engine plenty of information about what you need. One way to do this is to add several specific words to the search box.

Example:

Your teacher has asked you to find out if the Red Cross helped people during the Kobe earthquake in Japan. You log on to your computer and open your favorite search engine, such as Google or Yahoo. In the search box, you type *Earthquake Japan Kobe Red Cross.* As a result, you have a small number of sites that give you specific information about how the Red Cross helped during the Kobe earthquake.

Another way to search effectively is to search for a phrase. When you search for a phrase, you put quotation marks around the words. The search engine looks for exactly that phrase.

Example: "How to prepare for an earthquake."

Answer the questions by finding information on the Web. Follow the guidelines above to help you search more effectively. Write down the answers in complete sentences. Then bring them to class to share with other students.

1. How did the Red Cross help in the Kobe earthquake in Japan?
2. If there is an earthquake, what should you do? Hint: Try a phrase search.
3. How do you volunteer to work for the Red Cross or the Red Crescent?
4. Where is the Habitat for Humanity office closest to you?
5. Where is the Red Cross office closest to you?

The World of Work

5

Jamestown College of Higher Education

Application for Employment

Position: Student Leader, International Club

Personal Information

Name: _____   Student ID #: _____

Address: _____   Zip: _____

Telephone: (Home) _____   (Cell) _____   (E-mail) _____

This chapter is about finding jobs, completing applications correctly, and doing well in interviews. Reading 1 is about how most people get jobs—with the help of people they know. Reading 2 explains how to complete applications accurately. Reading 3 explains how to be successful in an interview.

In this chapter, you will practice:

Reading Skills
- ➡ Previewing a reading
- ➡ Predicting

Vocabulary Skills
- ➡ Using context clues to understand vocabulary
- ➡ Understanding present and past participle adjectives

Life Skills
- ➡ Understanding the importance of networking
- ➡ Completing applications
- ➡ Being successful in an interview

Before You Read

Previewing

Discuss the questions and complete the task. Work in small groups.

1. How do people find out about new jobs? List four ways to find out about a new job.

   a. _____

   b. _____

   c. _____

   d. _____

2. How do you think most people get their jobs?

3. Are you working? How did you find out about your job?

Using Context Clues to Understand Vocabulary

The words in bold print are in Reading 1. Guess the meaning of each word by looking at the context. Circle the letter of the best answer.

1. My **favorite** food is Mexican food. I enjoy cooking and eating this food more than other kinds of food.

   a. liked a little
   b. liked the best
   c. not liked very much

2. One way to find a new car for sale is to look in the **classified** section of the local newspaper. You'll find all kinds of cars for sale.

   a. the part of the newspaper where you can read about sports
   b. the part of the newspaper where you can find information about science
   c. the part of the newspaper that has advertisements for different things

3. The singer who won "American Idol" is very **promising.** I think he will be a great singer in the future.

   a. showing that someone is likely to be successful
   b. famous, known by a lot of people
   c. rich, has a lot of money

4. John **was promoted** to manager last week. He is happy that he now earns more money and that he still works for the same company. However, his new position is quite difficult.

   a. got a new job in a different company
   b. lost a job
   c. got a better job in the same company

5. My father is so **old-fashioned.** He doesn't like any of my clothes, and he thinks I should be in by ten o'clock at night. He needs to join the twenty-first century!

   a. not modern
   b. belonging to the present time
   c. looking forward to the future

Now Read

The Power of Networking

1   How do people find out about a new job? Here are four stories by college students.

Hiro: I am an international student, so I cannot work at most jobs. I am allowed to work part-time for the college, however. The tuition is very high for international students, and I wanted a job to help my parents pay for my education. We have a job board at school. I looked at the job board each day for a couple of weeks. It was depressing because there were no jobs available on campus. Then one day I saw an opening for a part-time job in the accounts office. I took down the job number and asked the employment adviser for an application. I completed it and had an interview a week later. Here I am! I enjoy the job, my father is happy I am paying part of the tuition, and I am improving my English.

Lisa: I was walking past one of my favorite clothing stores in the mall. I noticed a help wanted sign in the window. I went in and asked to see the manager. I told her I loved the store and that I bought most of my clothes there. She gave me an application and asked me to complete it and come in for an interview. Everything went well, and I've been working at the store for six months.

continued

Hussein: Every day I got the local paper and opened it to the classified pages. I looked for computer jobs. I circled the job openings that looked promising. I read the job advertisements very carefully. Most ads ask you to call for an application. I did this and completed the application as soon as I received it. If I didn't hear back from the company after a week, I called and asked about my application. One time I called and spoke to the manager. She asked me to come in for an interview. I've been working with this company for two years, and I've already had two promotions.

Tessa: All my friends know I am crazy about animals. One day at school, a friend told me her vet was looking for an assistant. The vet needed someone who knew a lot about animals. Well, that's me! I've grown up with cats, dogs, chickens, and horses! I knew this was great experience for the job, so I went in to see the vet. He was really busy because his receptionist was at lunch and the phone kept ringing. I asked if I could help. I answered the phone and greeted people with their animals that day. When the office closed, we talked about the job, and I told him how much I loved animals. I walked in to ask for an application form, and I walked out with a job!

continued

2   There are many ways to find a job, including newspaper advertisements, help wanted signs, and job boards. Online services through the Internet have also increased the opportunities to learn about new jobs. In fact, there are thousands of Web sites advertising jobs and offering help in applying for these jobs. Some services are free; others can be quite expensive. With all these opportunities for job finding, it is perhaps surprising to learn that about seventy-five percent of all people get their job the old-fashioned way—through someone they know. This is called *networking*.

3   *Networking* means meeting other people in order to share information and support each other. You know lots of people—friends, family, neighbors, co-workers, students, and teachers. These people are the beginning of your network. Ask them if they know of any job openings. The people you talk to can ask their friends. Thus, your network expands very quickly. If you ask twenty people, and each of the twenty asks another five people, then you are actually making one hundred enquiries about job openings. This is the strength of networking.

4   Networking not only helps people who are seeking employment, but also has advantages for the employer. Employers are usually much happier finding a new employee through someone they know. For one thing, it means they don't have to spend a lot of money advertising, which is very expensive. It also saves time. Moreover, if a good employee recommends a friend, the employer believes the friend is also likely to be a good employee. So networking helps everyone.

5   Most people usually do not limit themselves to just one way of finding a job. They may network with their friends and apply to advertisements in the newspaper, for example. Going online and checking which jobs are available is also good experience—even if you don't apply for any of these positions. Reading and talking about employment opportunities increases knowledge and experience, so when the right interview comes up, you'll be ready. Above all, remember, three out of every four people get their jobs through not only what they know, but who they know. Networking works.

After You Read

How Well Did You Read?

Work with a partner. Read the following statements. Write *T* (true), *F* (false), or *N* (not enough information).

_____ 1. You need a computer to find a job through networking.

_____ 2. Three of the four students got their jobs through networking.

_____ 3. Employers like to hire friends of their employees.

_____ 4. Tessa is studying to be a vet.

Check Your Understanding

Answer these questions in complete sentences.

1. How did Hussein find his job?

   _____

2. Why did the vet give Tessa a job?

   _____

3. Why does Hiro need to work?

   _____

4. Why was it more difficult for Hiro to get a job?

   _____

5. Why do you think the writer calls networking "old-fashioned"?

   _____

6. Why do employers usually prefer to hire through networking than by advertising?

   _____

Life Skill

Understanding the Importance of Networking

Networking is an important part of today's world. People network to find new jobs. They also network to find a good doctor, a good dentist, and a good school. Networking is about questions. First you ask people for help. Then you ask for more information.

To begin a networking conversation, you can say:

"I need a favor."

"I wonder if you could help me."

"I'd like to ask your advice about something."

Next, you ask the question:

"Do you know if there are any job openings in your company?"

"Do you have a good doctor?"

"Is your son doing well at his school? Are you pleased with your son's school?"

Then you can ask a follow-up question:

"Do you know someone I could call to ask about the job opening?"

"Where is your doctor's office?"

"Why do you think your son's school is good?"

Complete these conversations between friends. Answer the questions. Make sure your answers fit the questions. When you finish, practice the conversations with a partner.

1.

Your Friend	You
I wonder if you could help me. My daughter has a really bad toothache. Do you have a good dentist?	Yes, my dentist is great!
Where is his office?	
Oh, it's near the college? That's good, because I live two blocks away. My daughter is frightened of dentists. Is he gentle?	
It's good to know that he likes working with children. Do you have his telephone number?	
Well, don't worry. I can look him up in the yellow pages. What's his name?	
Dr. Mac . . . How do you spell that?	
McCloud. Thanks. I'll get his number and call him right away. I'll tell him you said he is a great dentist.	

2.

You	Your Friend
Hi, David. I wonder if you could do me a favor. I'm looking for a new job. Does your company have any job openings?	
I'm sorry to hear that business is bad. Do you know any company that has job openings right now?	
Yes, I know Cost Cut Foods. I shop there sometimes. I didn't know your wife works there. What kind of jobs do they have?	
I can't unload the trucks because I have a bad back, but I have experience as a cashier. I think I'll give them a call. Do you know the name of the person I should call?	
Bruce Parsons. Do you happen to have his number?	
Okay, call me tonight. Thanks a lot. Do you mind if I tell Mr. Parsons that I am a friend of your wife's?	
Employee of the year! That's great. I'll tell him I know you guys very well. Thanks again for your help, and I'll hear from you this evening.	

Understanding Present and Past Participle Adjectives

In Reading 1, Hiro says that the job board is "depressing." *Depressing* is the present participle form of the verb *depress*. English uses the present and past participle forms of some verbs as adjectives that describe emotions. The present participle ends in *-ing* (*exciting, boring*); the past participle ends in *-ed* (*excited, bored*).

Students are often confused by present and past participles. The past participle form describes the person who experiences the feeling.

> **Examples:**
>
> James is **bored.**
> The children are **excited.**

The present participle form describes the thing or person that makes someone feel this way.

> **Examples:**
>
> James is bored. Why? He's watching a **boring** movie.
> The children are excited. Why? They are playing an **exciting** game.

A. Read this list of common participial adjectives. If you don't know the meaning of a word, ask your teacher to explain it.

Participial Adjectives — Present	Participial Adjectives — Past
amazing	amazed
annoying	annoyed
boring	bored
confusing	confused
depressing	depressed
disappointing	disappointed
embarrassing	embarrassed
exciting	excited
frightening	frightened
frustrating	frustrated
shocking	shocked
surprising	surprised

B. Complete the sentences by choosing the correct form of the participle in parentheses ( ).

1. (annoy) Peter was _____ because the bus was late, and he missed his class.

2. (frighten) The movie *The Ring* was _____. I don't want to see it again.

3. (embarrass) Jane was _____ when the teacher asked her to answer the question. Jane gave the wrong answer, and the other students laughed at her.

4. (depress) The news on TV last night was very _____. All you hear on news programs is bad news.

5. (frustrate) Learning a second language can be _____. It's hard to learn new grammar and all those new words.

6. (confuse) This math problem is _____. I don't understand it at all. Could you explain it, please?

7. (disappoint) I was _____ when I failed my driver's test. I am a good driver, but I was just too nervous.

8. (bore) The history teacher was _____. He talked for hours in a quiet voice. Some students even fell asleep.

9. (shock) Some parents are _____ when they listen to the music teenagers like. The parents do not like this music at all.

10. (surprise) The students were _____ when the teacher said she did not give homework. They thought all teachers gave homework.

Part A: Tips on Completing Applications

Before You Read

Previewing

Work in small groups. Discuss the questions and complete the task.

1. What kinds of application forms are there? Write down some examples.

   a. _____

   b. _____

   c. _____

2. What kinds of application forms have you completed? Did you have any problems completing these forms?

Using Context Clues to Understand Vocabulary

These words are in Reading 2, Parts A and B. Find the words in the reading (in bold print). Read the sentences around the words carefully to get a general understanding of the word. Then match the words with the correct definitions.

Word	Definition
_____ 1. stage	a. difficult in an interesting way
_____ 2. impressed	b. do something without pay
_____ 3. challenging	c. not allowed by law
_____ 4. fired	d. a time or level in a long process
_____ 5. honest	e. made to feel admiration or respect
_____ 6. volunteer	f. truthful
_____ 7. illegal	g. made to leave a job

Now Read

Tips on Completing Applications: Part A

1   If the first stage of job hunting is finding a job to apply for, the second **stage** is completing an application. There are numerous ways to get an application form. Job hunters can pick one up from different businesses, write off for an application, request one by telephone, or complete one online. However you get the application, the forms are usually similar. They are quite easy to read and, with a little practice, relatively easy to fill out. You should always complete an application very carefully, as this is your first introduction to what could be a new job.

2   First of all, before you complete the application, you should write down all your personal information, your education history, and your employment background. Make sure that all the dates are correct and that the names and addresses are spelled accurately. Use these notes to complete the form. Write neatly and use an erasable pen. No one is **impressed** with an untidy application. If you pick up an application from a company, don't fill it out there and then. Take it home with you, so you have time to complete it carefully.

3   Applications are straightforward to complete if you have a perfect employment history. In this case "perfect" means that you have never been unemployed, you've never lost a job, and you have a good educational background and references. However, most people do not have a perfect employment history. Many people, for example, have lost a job through no fault of their own. Companies go out of business, and people lose work. Many others, especially women, have long periods of time when they are not working. People often need to retrain in new skills or, in the case of immigrants, learn a second language. Finally, what about all those people who are entering the work force for the first time and have no experience? How do they complete a form that asks for a job history? In many cases, therefore, applications can be **challenging** to complete.

continued

4   People often ask the following questions when completing an application:

1. What do I write down if I have never worked?

2. I was **fired** from my last job. Should I explain why or not write about this job at all?

3. I worked for five years and then moved to Canada and learned English. This took three years. What do I say about not working for three years?

4. I almost got a degree. I took college classes, but I never finished the degree. I even took some extra classes at a different college. Can I say that I got my degree?

5. I only have references from another country, from people who don't speak English. What should I do?

6. One application asked me how old I was. I was embarrassed because I am fifty-two. But I still need a job! Can I say I am only forty?

7. I am filling out an application. The form asks how much money I want as an hourly wage. I think if I ask for too much, the company will not interview me. If I ask for too little, they might pay me less than they were planning to. What do I write for this question?

Part B: Tips on Completing Applications

Before You Read

Predicting

Work with a partner. Chapter 3 talked about the importance of predicting, or guessing what the writer is going to say. Talk about the seven questions in Part A. How do you think the writer will answer these questions? Write down your answers.

1. _____
2. _____
3. _____
4. _____
5. _____
6. _____
7. _____

Now Read

Finish the reading. See if your answers to the questions are the same as the writer's answers.

Tips on Completing Applications: Part B

Before we look at each specific question, there are a couple of very important general points about completing applications. The employer needs to get an accurate picture of you. Don't try to hide anything and always be truthful. Remember: The employer checks references. If an employer finds out you have not told the truth, you will not get the job. Now, let's look at each specific question.

1. *What do I write down if I have never worked?*

   Getting a job without experience sometimes seems impossible. The job requires experience, but you can't get experience without a job. It's a vicious circle. Just

   continued

remember, however, that everyone starts without experience. So, don't be embarrassed about your lack of work experience. Instead think of other things you have done that have prepared you for the world of work. Have you been a volunteer? Have you been the leader of a club? Have you helped to organize a club or have you ever coached a sports team? In the space under employment history, write down your experiences in these areas. This experience is important.

2. *I was fired from my last job. Should I explain why or not write about this job at all?*

   You need to write about this job. If you don't, the employer will wonder what you were doing during this time. However, you do not need to write on the application form that you were fired. Under *reason for leaving*, you can write, "will explain at interview." Then, when you are in your interview you can explain what happened and, most importantly, what you have learned from the experience.

3. *I worked for five years and then moved to Canada and learned English. This took three years. What do I say about not working for three years?*

   Again, you need to be **honest**. You should not feel bad that you needed time to learn another language and get used to living in another country. Think of other things you did in those three years. Did you **volunteer** at your child's school? Did you remodel your house? Make sure the employer knows that you were busy during this time.

4. *I almost got a degree. I took college classes, but I never finished the degree. I even took some extra classes at a different college. Can I say that I got my degree?*

   No! Taking college classes and getting a degree are two different things. You must not exaggerate your education. You should feel good about the courses you took, and you can write about those. You don't need to say you didn't finish the degree. Write about what you learned.

5. *I only have references from another country, from people who don't speak English. What should I do?*

   It can be difficult to find a job if you don't have work references in the country where you are living. If you have a letter of reference written in your own language, ask someone to translate it. You should also think about people where you are living now. Think about your network. Is there someone else you could ask for a reference? What about your teacher, for example?

6. *One application asked me how old I was. I was embarrassed because I am fifty-two. But I still need a job! Can I say I am only forty?*

continued

This is an interesting question. It is actually **illegal** for an employer to ask for your date of birth. If this question is on an application, leave it blank. Employers are also not allowed to ask you about the following:

what you look like

your religion

if you are married

if you have children

your race

if you have any health problems (if the job needs someone to lift heavy things, the employer can ask if you have any health problems that will make lifting difficult)

7. *I am filling out an application. The form asks how much money I want as an hourly wage. I think if I ask for too much, the company will not interview me. If I ask for too little, they might pay me less than they were planning to. What do I write for this question?*

Money questions are difficult. If the application asks you how much you want to earn, write "open." This means you can talk about money in the interview. If the application asks how much money you earned in past jobs, you need to give a specific amount.

Applications open the door to a good job. So, prepare your personal information before you begin to fill one out, use an erasable pen, be honest, and make sure the employer knows you can do the job. One last tip: Make a copy of the application before you send it in. Before you go for an interview, you can read it again. This will help you prepare for the interview.

After You Read

How Well Did You Read?

Read the following statements. Write *T* (true), *F* (false), or *N* (not enough information).

_____ 1. Employers check references to make sure the employee has completed the application accurately.

_____ 2. You can't get a job without experience.

_____ 3. You should not write about volunteer experience.

_____ 4. Employers can ask any question they want.

Check Your Understanding

A. Circle the letter of the best answer.

1. The best way to complete an application is by _____.

    a. taking notes with you to the company and completing the application there
    b. preparing carefully and completing it at home
    c. preparing carefully and not answering difficult questions

2. *They are quite easy to read and, with a little practice, **relatively easy** to fill out.*

    Relatively easy means

    a. very easy.
    b. quite easy.
    c. not easy at all.

3. If a person has no job experience, can they write down some other experience on the application?

    a. Yes, because there are many kinds of experience.
    b. Yes, but they are not telling the truth.
    c. No, they must always leave this part of the application empty.

4. The writer believes that it is better to _____.

    a. write a letter explaining why you were fired from a job
    b. talk about this experience when you are at the interview
    c. forget about the job you lost

5. *No! Taking college classes and getting a degree are two different things. You must not **exaggerate** your education.*

    Exaggerate means

    a. tell the truth about something.
    b. keep quiet about something.
    c. make something sound better than it really is.

6. Which statement is accurate according to the reading?

    a. Employers can never ask about your health.
    b. Employers can sometimes ask about your age.
    c. Employers can never ask if you are single.

7. What should you write if the application asks about your salary at your last job?

    a. "open"
    b. how much you earned
    c. how much you want to earn in the new job

8. What is the topic of the last paragraph?

    a. completing applications
    b. helpful advice to complete applications
    c. being honest

B. Read these lists of words and phrases. Underline the word in each list which is a general description of the other words in the list. The first one is done for you.

online applications   untidy applications
telephone requests   application mistakes
going to companies   exaggerating education
<u>ways to get an application</u>   not telling the truth

previous jobs   previous jobs
education   volunteer
personal information   experience
address   basketball coach

reference
teacher
landlord
religious leader

C. Now read the general topics. Using information from the reading, write down three specific examples of the topic.

1. Tips on completing applications:

   _____

2. Serious mistakes in completing applications:

   _____

3. Questions an employer usually asks on an application:

   _____

4. Illegal questions:

   _____

5. Reasons why people find it difficult to complete applications:

   _____

How to Be Successful in an Interview

Before You Read

Previewing

Work in small groups. Discuss these questions and complete the task.

1. Have you ever had an interview? What happened? How did you feel during the interview? Did you get the job?

2. Many people get nervous in an interview. Why do you think people get nervous? What happens to your English when you get nervous?

3. What questions do people ask in interviews? Write three interview questions:

   a. _____?

   b. _____?

   c. _____?

Using Context Clues to Understand Vocabulary

These words are in Reading 3. Find the words in the reading (in bold print). Read the sentences around the words carefully to get a general understanding of the word. Then match the words with the correct definitions.

Word	Definition
_____ 1. stress	**a.** a liquid with a strong, pleasant smell
_____ 2. human nature	**b.** a person who is trying to get a new job
_____ 3. common	**c.** a person who works at the front desk in a company
_____ 4. applicant	**d.** feelings of worry about work or personal life
_____ 5. hurt someone's feelings	**e.** happening often
_____ 6. perfume/cologne	**f.** make someone feel upset or unhappy
_____ 7. receptionist	**g.** good and bad traits that all people have

Now Read

How to Be Successful in an Interview

1   If an application is the door to a new job, the interview is the key to opening that door. Almost everyone has an interview at some point in his or her adult life. Today, because many people change their jobs more often, people usually interview several times during their lives. Interviews make everyone nervous. Some people feel so nervous during an interview that they forget answers to even simple questions. This can be very frustrating—especially if you don't get the job. So what can you do to reduce **stress** during this very important time?

2   The first part of the answer is preparation. One reason people get nervous is because they don't know what to expect. In fact, it is **human nature** to fear the unknown. So, it makes sense that if you find out more information before the interview, you will be less nervous. Find out as much as you can about the job you are applying for. One way to do this is to go online. Use the title of the job as a key word for a search. You can also go to a career adviser and ask for more information. Next, you should find out about the company. How large is it? What does the company make or do? Again, going online to the company Web site will help you.

3   The next step is to prepare your answers. You don't know exactly which questions the interviewers will ask you, but there are several very **common** questions. The

continued

interviewers will probably ask you why you applied to that company. They will want to know why you want the job. Most important, they will want to know why they should hire you and not somebody else. You must prepare answers to these questions by using the information you have found online or in a library. You should also use the same information to write down three questions you have about the job or the company on a note card. You should bring these questions with you to the interview.

4   The interviewers have to choose one **applicant** for the job. They have to try to get to know each applicant during the interview. So they will ask some difficult questions to see which applicant gives the best answers. A common difficult question is "What are your strengths?" This is your chance to "sell yourself." The interviewer expects you to talk about all the things you are good at doing. First of all, you need to think about this question before the interview. Think of a few things you are good at doing. Perhaps you are good at working with people, and you are good at solving problems, for example. Be ready with your answer. If you feel uncomfortable talking about yourself, practice first in front of a mirror!

5   Another difficult question is "What are your weaknesses?" This is not your time to talk about how you find it difficult to get out of bed early on Monday mornings. Instead, you can say something like "I sometimes feel shy. I need to practice talking to a lot of people." Some applicants give an example of a mistake they made at another company. They explain what they learned from this mistake. For example, an applicant might say, "I like to do things quickly. In my last job, I worked with a person who was slow. One day I told her to hurry up, and this **hurt her feelings.** It was difficult to work with her for a while. Of course, I said I was sorry. I showed her how to work more quickly. I learned that you must choose your words carefully." Employers like to hear that you know you make mistakes but and that you can learn from these mistakes.

6   The interview day arrives. You know about the job and the company. You have practiced answering questions. You should always arrive early, so make sure you know exactly where the interview is. Dress sensibly. Avoid wearing heavy **perfume** or **cologne** since a lot of people today dislike strong smells. Some people are even allergic to heavy perfume. When you walk into the building, smile at the **receptionist.** This is usually the first person you see as you enter a company. Greet him or her nicely. Interviewers often ask their receptionists about the applicants. When you meet the interviewer, smile again. Managers often report that they hire people who smile rather than people who look nervous. Make sure your handshake is not too strong and not too weak. Sit down, take a deep breath, smile again, and you are ready.

7   Hopefully, the interviewer will ask you questions you have already practiced. If you don't understand a question, however, make sure you ask the interviewer to repeat it. You could say, "Excuse me, I didn't quite understand the question. Could you say it again?"

8   The last question of the interview is often "Do you have any questions?" Again, you are ready for this question. Take out your note card with your questions. This

continued

shows the interviewer you are organized. Always ask at least one question or the interviewer will think you are not interested in the job. You can ask a specific question about the job. You can also ask a general question like "What do your employees like best about this company?" or "Do you think this company is going to continue to grow in the future?" Finally, you should end by saying that you have enjoyed talking to the person and are very interested in the job. Ask, "When will you make a decision?" and then shake hands again, smile, and say good-bye.

9   If you prepared well, you should feel good when you leave the interview. You should know more about the company and the job, and the interviewer should know more about you. Remember to smile and talk to the receptionist as you leave the building. Later the same day, think about the questions and your answers. Think of how you could give better answers next time. Keep practicing because most people have several interviews before they get a job. Finally, when a manager calls you and offers you a job, let the manager know you are excited to work for him or her. "That's great!" you can say. "When can I start?"

After You Read

How Well Did You Read?

Read the statements. Write *T* (true), *F* (false), or *N* (not enough information).

_____ **1.** If an applicant finds out more information about the interview, he or she will be more nervous.

_____ **2.** The interviewer usually asks about ten questions—some difficult, some easy.

_____ **3.** When you answer the question "What are your weaknesses?" you should not tell the truth.

_____ **4.** The first person an applicant usually sees in a company is the interviewer.

Check Your Understanding

Answer the questions in complete sentences.

1. Why do some applicants feel frustrated after an interview?

    _____

2. Why do people usually feel better before an interview if they prepare first?

    _____

3. Paragraph 3 talks about common questions that interviewers ask. Write down, in question form, these three questions.

   a. _____

   b. _____

   c. _____

4. What does the expression "sell yourself" mean?

   _____

5. According to paragraph 5, what should you talk about if you give an example of a mistake you made in the past?

   _____

6. Who is often the first person you see when you walk into a company's building?

   _____

7. Give two examples of things you should do to make a good first impression.

   _____

8. Why should you always ask at least one question at the end of the interview?

   _____

9. You have finished the interview. You realize you gave a few very weak answers. How can you learn from this mistake?

   _____

10. How do applicants feel when they hear the interview was successful?

   _____

Understanding Present and Past Participle Adjectives

A. Choose a word to complete each sentence. In some sentences more than one answer is possible.

frightening	frightened	frustrating	frustrated
exciting	excited	embarrassing	embarrassed
disappointing	disappointed		

1. An interview can be _____ if you don't know what is going to happen.

2. The applicant was _____ when he heard he didn't get the job.

continued

3. I was _____ because I forgot the answer to a really simple question.

4. The interview was _____. I didn't know what the interviewer was talking about.

5. The whole experience of interviewing was _____ ! I enjoyed meeting the manager and answering his questions. I think I got the job!

B. Complete the sentences using your own words.

1. My first interview was embarrassing because _____.

2. My husband was disappointed when _____.

3. The manager was frustrated because _____.

4. Interviews can be frightening if _____.

5. Applicants who are learning English sometimes feel frustrated at an interview because _____.

Matching Questions with Answers

Work with a partner. Read the questions and the applicant's answers. Draw a line to show which answer matches each question.

1. Why do you want this job?

2. What are your greatest strengths?

3. What salary do you want to earn from us?

4. Do you prefer to work by yourself or with other people?

5. Being busy can be stressful. How do you reduce your stress?

a. I like to work in a group when we have to figure out a problem or get a new idea. But I also feel comfortable working by myself, especially if the work is difficult and I need to concentrate.

b. What salary is usually offered to the person in this job?

c. I am always on time, and I enjoy working. I like to be busy, and I love to learn new skills.

d. This job is perfect for me. I can use my skills and learn new things. I've read about the company and believe this is a very good place to work.

e. Everyone feels stress sometimes. I feel more stress when I am not busy! I like to walk during my lunch break, and I also make sure I smile a lot. That helps reduce stress.

Vocabulary Review

A. Choose the best word or words to complete each sentence.

favorite	relatively	boring	human nature
stress	promoted	honest	perfume
disappointed	applicants		

1. Please don't wear _____ in this class. I am allergic to strong smells.

2. If you feel a lot of _____, you should take a hot bath. This will relax you and make you feel better.

3. I was _____ because my husband forgot my birthday. Next year, I will make sure I tell him the week before!

4. I think this math class is _____ easy. However, my friends say the next class is really difficult.

5. Good news! My manager _____ me. I have a better job, and I'm earning more money!

6. This movie is _____. Let's turn it off and go to bed.

7. When the manager of the bookstore advertised for a new salesperson, more than twenty _____ called her to ask about the job.

8. When you complete an application, you must be _____. Don't exaggerate your experience or your education.

9. It is _____ to be afraid of things we don't understand. All people feel this way.

10. I know I'm old-fashioned, but my _____ singer is Elvis Presley! I just love his music!

B. Complete the sentences using your own words.

1. I looked in the classified section of the newspaper because I wanted _____

   _____.

2. Sometimes my little brother is very annoying because he _____

   _____.

continued

3. Juan was very embarrassed at the restaurant because he_____

_____.

4. Learning another language can be frustrating because _____

_____.

5. The restaurant manager fired Peter because he_____

_____.

6. When Hiroko first moved to America, she couldn't get used to_____

_____.

7. My friend hurt my feelings when she said she_____

_____.

8. This is an example of a common question an interviewer asks:_____

_____.

9. I was shocked when I heard that _____

_____.

10. It is embarrassing for students of English if they _____

_____.

Expanding the Topic

Connecting Reading with Writing

A. You are preparing for an interview. Here are some very common interview questions. Read the questions carefully, and write the answers in complete sentences. Use information and vocabulary you have learned in this chapter to make your answers interesting. When you finish, compare your answers with a partner.

1. Tell me about yourself.

2. Why do you want this job?

3. What are your greatest strengths?

4. Give me an example of a time you had a problem at work. What happened and what did you learn from this problem?

5. Someone you work with is not working as quickly as you are working. This person is slowing you down. What would you do?

6. What are your greatest weaknesses?

7. What salary do you want to earn here?

8. Why have you changed jobs so many times?

9. What are your future plans?

10. Do you have any questions?

B. Your college is advertising for a new leader for the International Student Club. You are very interested in the position. You think it will be good experience for you, and it pays ten dollars an hour. Because it is on campus, all students can apply. You pick up the following application. Read it carefully, and then complete the application.

Jamestown College of Higher Education

Application for Employment

Position: Student Leader, International Club

Personal Information

Name: _____   Student ID #: _____

Address: _____   Zip: _____

Telephone: (Home) _____   (Cell) _____   (E-mail) _____

Education (most recent first)

School	Address	Dates	Subjects studied / degrees
_____	_____	_____	_____
_____	_____	_____	_____
_____	_____	_____	_____
_____	_____	_____	_____

Activities at School

Please list the activities you have taken part in at school. Describe what you did in these activities.

1. _____

2. _____

continued

---

3. _____

4. _____

5. _____

Employment (most recent first)

Company name	Address	Dates	Position	Reason for leaving
_____	_____	_____	_____	_____
_____	_____	_____	_____	_____
_____	_____	_____	_____	_____
_____	_____	_____	_____	_____

Goals

What are your goals for the future? How will this job help you reach these goals?

_____

_____

_____

_____

Why should Jamestown College choose you for this position?

_____

_____

_____

_____

Signature: _____

Date: _____

Exploring Online

A. Go online. Do an advanced search to look for more examples of common interview questions. Bring these questions to class. Practice answering them with a partner.

B. Your teacher has asked you to make a list of things you should do in an interview and things you should not do. Go online. Do an advanced search to find information. Using this information, complete the following chart:

Do's and Don'ts of Interviewing

Do's	Don'ts
Be early.	Chew gum.
Say hello to the receptionist.	Answer a question with just a yes or a no.

CHAPTER

From One World to Another

This chapter is about traveling from one culture to a very different culture. Reading 1 describes some of the difficulties people can experience as they move to a new culture. The second reading discusses problems parents and teenagers experience when they move to a different country. The last reading is a short story set in the mid 1800s. It is about a young Chinese man who travels to the very different world of America in search of gold.

In this chapter, you will practice:

Reading Skills

➡ Previewing a reading

➡ Finding the main idea of a paragraph

➡ Expanding previewing skills

Vocabulary Skills

➡ Using context clues to understand vocabulary

➡ Previewing vocabulary

➡ Understanding the prefix *dis-*

Life Skills

➡ Asking for and giving advice

➡ Making compromises

Before You Read

Previewing

Work with a partner. Discuss the questions and complete the tasks.

1. Reading 1 is about how people feel when they first arrive in a new country. How did you feel when you first arrived in the country where you are now living? Make a list with your partner about how you felt in your first week or two.

   a. <u>I felt confused.</u>
   b. <u>I felt tired.</u>
   c. _____
   d. _____
   e. _____
   f. _____

2. What was confusing to you? Now make a list about what was confusing in the first week, and explain why it was confusing.

   a. <u>The language was confusing. I couldn't understand people.</u>
   b. _____
   c. _____
   d. _____
   e. _____

3. Do you still feel the same way? Do you feel differently now?

Using Context Clues to Understand Vocabulary

The words in bold print are in Reading 1. Guess the meanings of each word by looking at the context. Circle the letter of the best answer.

1. As children grow up, they learn about **acceptable behavior** from their parents and other people around them. When they behave in an acceptable way, people around them are happy; if they behave in an unacceptable way, people get angry or sad.

   a. behavior that most people think is okay
   b. behavior that most people think is rude
   c. the way all children behave

continued

2. Many students experience **emotional anxiety** before an important test.

   a. a feeling of excitement
   b. a feeling of nervousness
   c. a feeling of great happiness

3. It's very interesting watching how dogs **interact** with one another. When they first meet, each dog sniffs the other but keeps a few inches away. As they get more used to each other, tails start wagging, and they begin to relax.

   a. smell something
   b. behave when around another person or animal
   c. talk to another person or animal

4. People often like watching **reality** TV shows like "Survivor" or "American Idol." People like to watch ordinary people do unusual or exciting things.

   a. unusual
   b. exciting
   c. based on everyday life

5. My friend always **criticizes** my driving. She says I'm driving too fast or I'm too close to the car in front. I get a little annoyed because she can't even drive.

   a. talks about what you do wrong
   b. explains how to do something
   c. points out the good things you do

Now Read

Culture Shock

1   Culture is the ideas, beliefs, and customs that are shared and accepted by people in a society. You are not born with culture; you learn it as you grow up. You learn your native language and listen to local music. You learn how to greet people and how, or how not, to ask for things you need. You enjoy food prepared in a certain way. You learn acceptable behavior by watching how other children and adults interact. You listen to people all around you, and you pick up the ideas and beliefs of those people. You are comfortable with this culture because it is familiar, and you understand it.

2   Then you decide to travel to another country that has a very different culture. You step into a completely different world. It's colder, and the air smells different. People walk more quickly and look a little strange. You've studied the language of this country at school for years, but you can't understand it. All the familiar parts of

continued

your life, the culture which you have absorbed since you were born, have disappeared with a snap of the fingers. It is no wonder, then, that many travelers experience culture shock—the physical and emotional anxiety you feel when moving to a different culture.

3   Culture shock has several stages. The first stage is often called the "honeymoon" stage. During this stage, everything around you is new and exciting. You are fascinated by the different ways people behave in this new culture. Everyone is very kind to you. The staff at your hotel is very friendly and helpful. Your host family or friends take you to lots of interesting places. It's like being on vacation. You're having a great time. Culture shock? No way. You are enjoying yourself too much to be suffering from culture shock.

4   The honeymoon stage can last from several days to several months. At some point, however, reality hits. This is the start of the second stage of culture shock, which for some people can be the most difficult. You realize you are not on vacation. You are not a visitor. You are going to live in this new country for a long time. People around you are less friendly. Your friends don't call you every day, and you have moved out of the hotel into an apartment. Your host family has stopped

continued

treating you like a special guest. Life becomes more difficult. You have to go shopping. This involves transportation. Which bus do you catch? How much does it cost?

5   In this second stage, the new culture no longer excites you. In fact, everything around you becomes frustrating. You are tired of listening to the new language and struggling to complete everyday tasks that were so uncomplicated in your native country. You begin to think everyone is making life difficult for you. You start to criticize people around you. Everyone around you is doing things wrong. You begin to stereotype, or make general judgments about, the people around you: "People in this country only think about themselves." "Everyone's lazy." "I just don't like them." "These people only care about money." This stage can be a depressing time.

6   Even when life is difficult, it goes on. Just as you learned your native culture growing up in your first country, you begin to learn the new culture. This is the beginning of the third stage. Life starts to get better. Your language skills improve, and everyday tasks become more familiar and therefore easier. You begin to recognize people on the bus you catch every day to school, and some of these people smile at you. The city becomes more familiar, and you learn about the best stores. You stop offering dollar bills every time you purchase something because you can now count change. You still think in your first language, but the new language doesn't give you such a headache. In this third stage, you feel as if you are beginning to belong. You will still have some bad days, but life is generally improving. You no longer feel like a fish out of water.

7   The final stage in culture shock is when you feel you belong where you are living. This does not mean you have forgotten your previous country. It means that you feel comfortable living in the new culture. You can now look at this culture objectively, seeing both the good things it has to offer and the bad things. You understand your earlier stereotypes were the result of not understanding. Understanding the new culture helps you to think more about your own culture and to understand more about yourself.

8   Culture shock can be really challenging for some people, especially the second stage, which is sometimes called the crisis, or most difficult, stage. However, there are many benefits of traveling to different cultures and learning about different ideas, beliefs, and customs. If you understand culture shock and its stages, traveling becomes even more enjoyable.

After You Read

How Well Did You Read?

Work with a partner. Read the statements. Write *T* (true), *F* (false), or *N* (not enough information).

_____ **1.** Culture is something you learn, not something you are born with.

_____ **2.** Every traveler experiences culture shock in the same way.

_____ **3.** The average length of culture shock is six months.

_____ **4.** The second stage of culture shock is probably the most difficult.

Discussing the Reading

Work in small groups. Talk about the questions.

1. Did you experience the "honeymoon" stage when you first arrived in a new country? What did you find fascinating about the new culture? How long did this stage last?

2. Are you still experiencing culture shock? If so, what stage do you think you are in? Explain how you feel to your group.

3. According to this reading, there are many advantages to getting to know another culture—even if you have to go through culture shock. What are the advantages of traveling to different cultures?

4. Paragraph 8 says that living in a new culture helps you understand more about yourself. Do you agree? If so, what have you learned about yourself by traveling?

Check Your Understanding

Circle the letter of the best answer.

1. What is the topic of this reading?

    a. culture shock
    b. the problems of culture shock
    c. the different stages of culture shock

2. How do you become comfortable with your native culture, according to this reading?

    a. You are born with your native culture, so it is easy for you to understand it.
    b. You begin to learn about your native culture from the time you are born.
    c. Your parents teach you everything about your native culture.

continued

3. *All the familiar parts of your life, the culture which you have **absorbed** since you were born, have disappeared with a snap of the fingers.*

   Absorbed means

   a. enjoyed.
   b. disliked.
   c. learned.

4. How does someone look at the new culture during the honeymoon stage?

   a. "I don't like the way people behave here."
   b. "This is cool! Everything is different here!"
   c. "I miss my family. I wish I could go home."

5. In the second stage of culture shock, "reality hits" the traveler. What does this expression mean?

   a. The traveler understands he or she is on vacation in this new country.
   b. The traveler thinks life in this new country is interesting.
   c. The traveler realizes that life in the new country will not be as easy as life at home.

6. How does a person look at people in the second stage of culture shock?

   a. "People are different here, but they are still nice."
   b. "Nobody here is even trying to understand me."
   c. "Most people are nice, but some are really unfriendly."

7. Which of these statements is an example of a stereotype?

   a. "A lot of people in this country work really hard."
   b. "I think people in this country care more about money than family."
   c. "Some of the students in my class are really lazy."

8. What would be a good title for paragraph 7?

   a. The Difficulties of Life
   b. Improving Your Language
   c. The Third Stage of Culture Shock

9. *You no longer feel like a fish out of water.*

   This means

   a. you feel thirsty all the time.
   b. you feel more comfortable.
   c. you feel very uncomfortable.

10. Which statement is correct according to paragraph 8?

    a. In the final stage of culture shock, you think the new culture is better than your native culture.
    b. In this last stage, you can't remember your native culture.
    c. In this stage you see both positive and negative things about life in the new culture.

Finding the Main Idea of a Paragraph

In previous chapters, you learned how to find the topic of a paragraph. The topic is the general idea of a paragraph. As your reading improves, it is important to understand the main idea of a paragraph. The main idea is similar to the topic, but it is more specific. Every paragraph usually has a main idea. You find the main idea by asking two questions:

- What is the general topic of the paragraph?
- What does the writer say about this topic?

The topic is usually a phrase—it is not a complete sentence. The main idea is a complete sentence.

Example:

Reread the first paragraph of Reading 1 on page 132.

What is the general topic? "Culture Shock" (phrase)

What does the writer say about culture? *"You are not born with culture; you learn about it as you grow up."*

This sentence expresses the main idea.

[Close skill box]

A. Work with a partner. Reread these paragraphs from Reading 1. As you read, ask yourself:
- What is the general topic of this paragraph?
- What does the writer say about this topic?

Then circle the letter of the best answer. The first one is done for you.

1.   Culture shock has several stages. The first stage is often called the "honeymoon" stage. During this stage, everything around you is new and exciting. You are fascinated by the different ways people behave in this new culture. Everyone is very kind to you. The staff at your hotel is very friendly and helpful. Your host family or friends take you to lots of interesting places. It's like being on vacation. You're having a great time. Culture shock? No way. You are enjoying yourself too much to be suffering from culture shock.

What is the main idea of this paragraph?

a. Everyone is kind to you during the first stage of culture shock.
b. the honeymoon stage of culture shock
c. In the first stage of culture shock, everything around you is new and exciting.

continued

2.   The honeymoon stage can last for several days to several months. At some point, however, reality hits. This is the start of the second stage of culture shock, which for some people can be the most difficult. You realize you are not on vacation. You are not a visitor. You are going to live in this new country for a long time. People around you are less friendly. Your friends don't call you every day, and you have moved out of the hotel into an apartment. Your host family has stopped treating you like a special guest. Life becomes more difficult. You have to go shopping. This involves transportation. Which bus do you catch? How much does it cost?

What is the main idea of this paragraph?

a. the second stage of culture shock
b. The second stage of culture shock is very difficult for some people.
c. In the second stage of culture shock, your friends don't call you very often.

3.   In this second stage, the new culture no longer excites you. In fact, everything around you becomes frustrating. You are tired of listening to the new language and struggling to complete everyday tasks that were so uncomplicated in your native country. You begin to think everyone is making life difficult for you. You start to criticize people around you. Everyone around you is doing things wrong. You begin to stereotype, or make general judgments about, the people around you: "People in this country only think about themselves." "Everyone's lazy." "I just don't like them." "These people only care about money." This stage can be a depressing time.

What is the main idea of this paragraph?

a. Life is frustrating.
b. People stereotype the people around them in the second stage.
c. In the second stage of culture shock, everything around you is frustrating.

4. The final stage in culture shock is when you feel you belong where you are living. This does not mean you have forgotten your previous country. It means that you feel comfortable living in the new culture. You can now look at this culture objectively, seeing both the good things it has to offer and the bad things. You understand your earlier stereotypes were the result of not understanding. Understanding the new culture helps you to think more about your own culture and to understand more about yourself.

What is the main idea of this paragraph?

a. feeling like you belong in the new country
b. In the final stage, you understand your own culture.
c. In the final stage, you feel like you belong in the new culture.

Life Skill

Asking for and Giving Advice

Reading 1 is about problems people experience during culture shock. During this time, or whenever we have a problem, we often ask for advice. We ask our friends, family, or teachers to tell us what we should do about a problem. In the same way, people often ask you to give advice. They want you to help them with their problems. There are several ways in English to ask for and offer advice:

If you want advice from a friend, you can say,

"I've got a problem. (Explain the problem.) What should I do?"

To give advice, you can use these modals:

must:	"You must go to the doctor's immediately." (very strong advice)
should:	"You should speak to the manager of the store." (strong advice)
ought to:	"You ought to go to the dentist and have that tooth checked." (good idea)
could:	"You could try the library. Maybe it will have the book you're looking for." (just a suggestion)

Work with a partner. Read these paragraphs about students of English who are experiencing culture shock. Then answer the questions using information from Reading 1 to help you. Use complete sentences.

1.   My name is Thuy and I come from Vietnam. I have been in America for several months now. Before I came here, I thought America would be wonderful. I thought I would go to a really great school and everyone would be very friendly. But life isn't like that. Now I know the truth about this country. Schools are not as good here as they were in my native country. The teachers let the students talk too much. I can't hear what the teacher is saying, and I don't want to hear what the students think. No one is friendly here. People say "Have a nice day," but they don't mean it. The other day, another student said "How's it going?" to me. I began to tell her I missed my country, but she had already walked away. People are rude here. No one was rude in my native country. I wish I could go home tomorrow.

What stage of culture shock do you think Thuy is in? _____

What makes you think this? _____

_____

What should Thuy do? Think of some things that Thuy can do to make herself happier.

Thuy must _____.

She should _____.

She ought to _____.

She could _____.

2.   My name is Jason. I've just arrived here to study engineering. I come from South Korea, and I've never traveled before. I feel so lucky to have this wonderful opportunity. I think this place is fantastic! The people here are really friendly. My host family takes me to a different place every day, so I'm really seeing a lot of the city. Even my teacher at college took me to the library when I couldn't find a book. Everyone's so nice! My only problem is that I'm so excited I can't sleep very well. But my teacher doesn't mind. I wish I could stay here forever.

What stage of culture shock is Jason in? _____

What makes you think this? _____

_____

What should Jason do?

Jason must _____.

He should _____.

He ought to _____.

He could _____.

3.   My name is Victor and I come from El Salvador. I've been here six months. When I first came here, I had a difficult time. I didn't like living here, and I wanted to go home. Now I feel more comfortable. My English is much better. I understand the culture better. However, I don't have any friends. I go to an English class, but I am very shy. I'm too nervous to talk with Americans because a lot of them don't understand my accent. Most of them are nice, but they just can't understand me. Sometimes I really like it here and think it is a great opportunity. Other days I wake up and feel depressed. I don't know why I still feel bad.

What stage of culture shock is Victor in? _____

What makes you think this? _____

_____

What should Victor do?

Victor must _____.

He should _____.

He ought to _____.

He could _____.

Caught Between Two Worlds

Before You Read

<table>
<tr><td>**Reading Skill**
</td><td>*Expanding Previewing Skills*

In Chapter 1, you learned that previewing gives you a general idea of what you are going to read. This helps you understand the reading more easily. You preview by reading the title and looking at any illustrations. Sometimes, however, just doing this is not enough to give you a general idea. Another way to preview is to read the title of the reading and the first sentence of each of the first few paragraphs. This will give you a more detailed idea of the reading.</td></tr>
</table>

Work in small groups. Discuss the questions and complete the task.

1. Read the title and the first sentence of the first four paragraphs (paragraphs 1–4) of Reading 2 on pages 144 and 145. What do you think this article is going to be about?

2. It's not easy being a teenager or a parent of a teenager. Teenagers and parents argue and fight over many things. What do you think they argue over the most? Make a list of these things.

    a. _____

    b. _____

    c. _____

    d. _____

    e. _____

3. What were you like when you were about sixteen years old? Did you argue with your parents? What kind of things did you argue about?

4. Do you think your parents' rules are still good rules for teenagers today? Explain your answer.

5. How does culture affect the way parents and teenagers behave together? What happens when a family moves from one culture to a different culture and the teenagers grow up in a new culture?

Previewing Vocabulary

Read the sentences carefully. Underline the word or words in the second sentence that mean the same as the word in bold print in the first sentence. The first one is done for you.

1. Animals **adapt** to cold weather in different ways. They <u>change their appearance and their behavior.</u> Some change the color of their fur, while others sleep through the winter.

2. **Adolescence** begins at about the age of twelve and continues until a person is an adult. These teenage years can be very difficult.

3. I have only two **rules** in this classroom: Try hard, and do your own work. If you follow these guidelines, you will be successful in this class.

4. There is **conflict** in several parts of the world. People continue to have disagreements about important things such as land, government, and religion.

5. Television can be a bad **influence** on children. It often has a negative effect on their behavior.

6. My mother **criticized** my cooking. She pointed out things that were wrong with the dinner: I used too much salt, I forgot the butter, and I cooked the dish for too long.

7. When it is very hot, you must **protect** yourself from the sun. You should look after yourself by staying out of the sun and drinking lots of water.

8. "I **refuse** to say I am sorry," said the young boy. "I am not sorry, so I will not say I am sorry."

Caught Between Two Worlds

1   Teenage years are challenging—for teenagers and parents. It is a time for teenagers to break away from their family and to begin to make a life for themselves. It is a time when parents need to let go of their children and recognize that their role has changed forever. Adolescence is therefore difficult for all families, but it is particularly challenging for immigrant families. In these families, teenagers and parents struggle with the adolescent years while also trying to adapt to an unfamiliar culture.

2   Many cultures have very clear rules to guide teenagers through these years. There are clear rules, for example, about what is acceptable for a girl to wear and about dating. A daughter is not allowed to go out in the evening unless she is with her brother or cousin. She must wear certain traditional clothes. A son knows he must come home by a specific time. Teenagers understand this because they have grown up with these cultural rules. However, what happens to these rules when the family moves to a different country with a different culture? Do the cultural rules and expectations of the native culture still apply?

continued

3   Many immigrant parents would answer yes. They need these rules to protect their children from the dangers of the new culture. Moreover, these rules worked for them when they were teenagers. So why shouldn't they work for their children?

4   Many teenagers, however, have a different answer. They, too, have grown up in their native culture, and the rules and expectations are very important to them. However, they are now learning a new culture and probably learning it faster than their parents. The old rules do not work in the new culture. Freedom is very important in the new culture: freedom to question teachers and parents, to take personal responsibility, to make and learn from mistakes. Teenagers from immigrant families quickly learn there are no clear rules about being a teenager in this culture. Girls have boys as friends, but may or may not have a "boyfriend." If a teen is dating, there are no strict rules about how to behave—even about sex. Life outside the home is complicated, and the old rules do not help.

5   Lien's family provides an example of the conflict that can develop between family members during this time. The family moved to the States from Vietnam when she was ten. Her father was a car mechanic in Vietnam. They lived in a nice house and had a comfortable life. Her parents believed, however, that Lien and her twin brother Thu would have more opportunities in America. So, like many immigrant parents, they moved to a different country because of their children. "This is all for you and your brother," the mother has told Lien several times a week since they arrived.

6   Lien was excited when she first arrived in Boston, but she soon found that life was not easy in America. Her father got a job, but he hated it. Her mother stayed in their apartment cooking traditional Vietnamese food for the evening meal. They didn't make any American friends. Lien quickly learned English, but her parents found it very difficult. They only spoke Vietnamese at home. When Lien's father was sick, Lien had to go to the doctor with him and explain what was wrong. This was very embarrassing for Lien and her father. At the grocery store, Lien's mother nervously stood behind her young daughter. Life was difficult, but the family was strong and stayed together. Everyone worked hard.

7   Things changed, however, when Lien and her brother Thu turned fifteen and went to high school. Thu made new friends with a group of teenagers. He got a job at a local store and used this money to buy baggy pants and sweatshirts. He grew his hair and pierced one ear so he could wear an earring. He started to go out at night and didn't want to tell his parents where he was going. His parents were constantly fighting with him. They didn't like his clothes or his friends. "Why are you wearing those clothes? You look like a gang member," his mother would cry. "You shouldn't be with those other boys," his father would say. "They are a bad influence on you. You need to stay in and study. We came here for you and your sister, remember?"

continued

8   Lien was caught in the middle of two worlds. She understood why her parents were worried, but she also understood that her brother wanted to be a teenager like the other kids his age. She too wanted more freedom, but she didn't dare challenge her parents like her brother. As the family arguments became louder, Lien became quieter. She covered her ears in her bedroom as she heard her brother shout, "You don't understand! You're living in the old world. Just leave me alone."

9   Thu finally left home in his last year of high school. He didn't finish school. Lien's parents disowned him; they refused to talk about him. They said to Lien, "This is all for you, Lien. You must work hard and do well." Lien wanted to explain to her parents that she, too, needed some freedom, but she didn't want any more fighting. So she kept quiet and worked hard.

10   Of course, many immigrant families live through the teenage years without breaking up like Lien's family. However, most families experience some conflict during these years. Few parents can say they have never heard their teenage children saying, "You don't understand." Most parents say they often don't understand their teenagers. So what can parents do during this difficult time to help themselves and their children?

continued

11   Experts have several suggestions. Parents shouldn't stereotype teenagers. Their clothes might be strange, but this does not mean they are bad kids. Second, teenagers do not like to be told to do things, but this does not mean they do not like rules. In fact, most teenagers feel more comfortable if there are rules to help them behave. Parents and teenagers must talk about these rules. They should listen to each other and compromise. For example, if the teenager wants to come home at 2:00 a.m., and the parents want him home by 10:00 p.m., they can compromise on 12:00. Finally, it's easy to criticize teenagers too much. Teenagers make a lot of mistakes, but that is part of growing up. Parents, however, must never only criticize. Instead, they need to praise the teens and look for positive things in their behavior.

12   It is difficult for immigrant teenagers to have one foot in the traditional world represented by their home and their family and the other foot in the "new" world of their friends and school. These teens often talk about living in an "in-between" place—feeling comfortable in neither the traditional nor the new world. In these situations teenagers and their parents need to seek advice from people who have experience and knowledge of trying to raise teenagers in a second culture.

After You Read

How Well Did You Read?

Read the following statements. Write *T* (true), *F* (false), or *N* (not enough information).

_____ **1.** Rules from one culture are not always helpful in a different culture.

_____ **2.** Teenagers believe the rules from their native country are not important.

_____ **3.** Thu was a member of a gang.

_____ **4.** Teenagers hate rules because they want freedom.

Discussing the Reading

Work in small groups. Talk about the questions.

1. Are teenage years always difficult for parents and children? Do you think the teenagers in Reading 2 are like most teenagers?

2. Why does Thu think that his parents don't understand him? Did you ever feel like this with your parents?

3. Lien's parents often remind her that they came to America to give her better opportunities. How do you think this makes Lien feel?

4. Do you agree that parents and teenagers should compromise about rules? Explain your answer.

Check Your Understanding

A. Circle the letter of the best answer.

1. What is the main idea of this reading?

    a. Teenage years are very challenging for both teenagers and their parents.
    b. Immigrant parents need to help their teenagers feel comfortable in the new culture.
    c. Adolescence is especially difficult for immigrant parents and teenagers.

2. What is the main idea of paragraph 2?

    a. cultural rules about adolescence
    b. Many cultures have rules that help teenagers through adolescence.
    c. Rules from one culture do not work very well in a different culture.

3. What is the main idea of paragraph 3?

    a. Immigrant parents agree.
    b. Immigrant parents want to protect their children.
    c. Immigrant parents think cultural rules from the native country can help their children in the new country.

4. What is the main idea of paragraph 4?

    a. Most immigrant teenagers think that freedom is very important.
    b. Most immigrant teenagers don't understand the new culture.
    c. Most immigrant teenagers believe that the old rules are not helpful.

5. What is the main idea of paragraph 11?

    a. Teenagers and parents must compromise over rules.
    b. There are several things parents can do to help their family through adolescence.
    c. Parents shouldn't stereotype teenagers, and they shouldn't criticize them all the time.

B. Answer the questions in complete sentences. Try to use your own words as much as possible.

1. Why is this article called "Caught Between Two Worlds"?

   _____

2. Why do many immigrant parents want their children to obey rules from their native culture?

   _____

3. This reading states that there are no clear rules about being a teenager in this new culture. What does this mean?

   _____

4. Why do you think the writer tells the story about Lien and her family?

_____

5. What does Thu mean when he says that his parents do not understand him?

_____

6. Paragraph 8 says that Lien was "caught in the middle." What does this mean?

_____

7. Why did Thu's family disown him?

_____

8. What is this statement an example of: "Kids who wear baggy pants are in gangs"?

_____

9. What example of a compromise does the writer give?

_____

10. According to this article, how do most immigrant teenagers feel about their traditional culture and their new culture?

_____

C. Work with a partner. Read the sentences about people in Reading 2. Each person asks for your advice. What advice would you give?

1. You are Thu's friend. He comes to you and says, "I've got to leave home. My parents are impossible. They don't understand me at all. They're just old country, and they will never accept that I am different from them. What should I do?"

   "I think you should _____

   _____."

2. You are Lien's friend. You are worried about her because she is very quiet and works too hard. You know about her problems at home. What advice would you give Lien?

   "Lien, I think you must _____

   _____."

continued

3. You are a friend of Lien and Thu's parents. They tell you about their problems with Thu. Your children are now adults and married. What advice would you give Lien's parents? "_____

_____."

Making Compromises

Thu and his family had problems because they could not communicate with each other. Experts suggest that an important part of communicating with anyone is making compromises. A **compromise** is when two people reach an agreement on a subject they did not at first agree upon. In a compromise, both people agree on less than they first wanted.

Example:

Teacher:	Your homework is due Wednesday.
Student:	Excuse me. Our math teacher has given us a lot of homework, and we have a chemistry test tomorrow. Could we turn in your homework next Monday? That will give us enough time to do a good job.
Teacher:	Well, I need it before Monday because I like to grade it over the weekend. Okay, turn it in on Friday by 4:00. That should give you enough time.
Problem:	The teacher wants the students' homework by Wednesday; the students want to turn it in the following Monday.
Compromise:	They will turn it in on Friday by 4:00.

In the table, you will read about arguments between parents and their teenage children. First, identify the problem. Then talk about these problems and discuss possible compromises. Write your answers in the space provided.

Parent's View	Teen's View	Problem	Possible Compromise
Mark is always asking for money. He gets an allowance but wants more. If he does more chores, we'll increase his allowance. However, he refuses to do more. He's lazy. He'll just have to do without until he is old enough to work.	My parents only give me an allowance of five dollars a week—and I'm fourteen! I need at least twenty bucks a week. That's what my friends get. I do everything my parents ask me to do. They want me to help more around the house, but I'm really busy. I have a lot of homework, and I play on the school football team.		
Elena is only seventeen —but she wants to act like she is twenty-five. She just got her driver's license and wants to use my car all the time. She doesn't understand that I need it. She also doesn't think about the cost of gas. What's worse, she never even tells me where she's going. I'm not going to let her use the car again until she grows up.	My mom refuses to let me use her car even though I've just passed my test. She doesn't understand I need it to get around. My friends live miles away, and we like to study together in the evenings. It's so boring where we live. There's nothing to do. She complains about the cost of gas, but I've got no money. She's the one earning so she should pay for the gas. That's what nice parents do.		

continued

Parent's View	Teen's View	Problem	Possible Compromise
My father started this family construction business fifty years ago. I've worked in it since I was a teenager. It's a good business. Now my son doesn't want to be part of it. He says he wants to design clothes. What sort of job is that? He wants to go to college, which is okay with me, but he must study business, not design. If he won't study business, I will not pay his tuition.	All my life my dad has said that I will follow him in the family business. This is the last thing I want to do. I love art and design. My dream is to be a famous designer and to have women wear my clothes. I know I can do it. I want to get along with my dad, but he's impossible. He's refusing to pay for college unless he gets his way. Well, I'm not giving up on my dream. I'll leave home if I have to.		

Before You Read

Previewing Vocabulary

These words are in Reading 3. Read the words and their definitions. Then choose the best word to complete each sentence.

Words	Definitions
exhaustion	a feeling of being extremely tired
dizzy	a feeling of not being able to balance yourself, especially after spinning around
crop	fruit or vegetables that a farmer grows
familiar	easy for you to recognize because you have seen it or heard it before
seeds	small, hard objects from which plants grow
confidently	with a feeling that you can do something well
ancestors	someone in your family who lived a very long time ago
disgust	a strong feeling of dislike and disapproval

1. My _____ come from Germany. My great, great grandfather came to Canada when he was a young boy.

2. The heavy snowstorm damaged the _____ of oranges.

3. You look _____ to me. Have I met you before?

4. Birds carry some _____ from one place to another. This helps plants to grow.

5. My sister changed the flat tire _____. She has changed lots of flat tires before.

6. The mountain climbers were suffering from _____. It was a very hard climb, and the weather was bad.

7. I was in bed for two days with the flu. Every time I tried to get out of bed, I felt _____.

8. The teacher looked at the boy's homework in _____. "This homework is much too short and much too untidy. Do it again, and take more care this time."

Now Read

Welcome to Gum Shan

1   Lu Yang sat back on his heels and rubbed his face, trying to wipe the exhaustion and hunger away. His eyes rested on the many rocks the latest rains had brought down from the hillsides onto the already rocky earth his family depended on. Two *mus*[1] of land—not enough to feed a husband and wife, let alone a family of five. Last year his father leased more land, but the landlord took back that land when rains destroyed the winter crop. As Lu Yang rested, the rain began again hard and cold. Lu Yang sighed as he watched more of the thin topsoil begin to wash away— red streams rushing down the hillside. He stood up and called down to his brothers, "Faster! Build up the wall. The rain's coming again!" His two younger brothers were piling up large stones to build a dam across the path of the draining water. The dam trapped the escaping topsoil, but allowed the water to drain through. When the rain stopped and the land dried, the boys would carry the topsoil back up the hillside where they would spread it over the land again. There it would stay until the next rain took it on another journey.

2   That night, while the family was sitting around the warm stove and eating small bowls of rice and salted vegetables, a visitor knocked on the door. It was Lu Yang's cousin Ah Min. Ah Min politely greeted his uncle and accepted some rice. Lu Yang could see his cousin was excited by the way his eyes danced in the firelight, but Ah Min had to wait for his uncle to ask him the news. And what news it was! An herbalist[2] had visited Ah Min's village two days before with news from Guangzhou, the great port where ships left and returned from the lands across the sea. People in a place called California had found gold! More gold than a man could carry! It was there, lying on the ground waiting to be picked up! Gum Shan—the Mountain of Gold—was calling anyone who was listening. Already a ship full of young men from villages near Ah Min's home had left for Gum Shan.

3   As Lu Yang listened, his heart began to race. He could hear it pounding even louder than the steady beat of the rain on the roof. This was the answer to his prayers! He saw his father quickly look over at him, and he knew his father was thinking the same. The large jars of vegetables, rice, and soybeans were already half empty, and there were many more months before spring arrived. Two days before, his father had quietly explained that there was not enough money for a bride-price to pay for the girl his family wanted Lu Yang to marry. They had to save the money to buy more seed, his father had said. Maybe next year. But now, Gum Shan would save the family.

[1] *mus:* a small piece of land used for growing crops

[2] **herbalist:** a person who uses plants as medicine

continued

4   Lu Yang's father stood up and pulled aside a woven rug that covered a small door in the floor. As his family watched silently, he raised the door and reached down into the dark space below. Pulling out a large food jar, he again reached down and this time retrieved a much smaller jar. It was old and cracked. It was no good for storing seeds because the air could pass through the cracks. The robbers that thundered through the villages every few months would not be interested in this jar. If they found the hiding space, they would take the larger one that was full of soybeans. Inside the smaller jar was a leather pouch. The family held its breath while the father carefully pulled out several coins. These had been Lu Yang's bride-price, but they were now to be saved for spring seed. The father took several coins and handed them to Lu Yang. His mother began to disagree with what her husband was doing, but he silenced her. She lowered her eyes as Lu Yang folded his fingers around the money.

5   "Go," his father said quietly. "Go to this Gold Mountain. Work hard. Save your gold and send it home. Then when we have enough for ten mus, seed, and cows, come back. Do not fall in love with the Mountain. True gold is here in your home with your family and your ancestors. We will wait for you to return. Go quietly now with your cousin. The rain will hide your footsteps. If the soldiers come, we will tell them you left to find work in Guangzhou."

6   Lu Yang knew why his father wanted him to leave while the rains were so heavy. The soldiers never came to the village in bad weather. There was good reason to fear these soldiers. No one was allowed to leave Guangzhou Province for foreign lands. The Emperor[3] needed young men for his army. If the soldiers caught a man trying to leave on a ship, they would kill him and place his head on a tall stick as a warning to others. There was always danger in leaving, but Lu Yang knew the choice for his family was worse. And the excitement in his stomach told him more: He wanted to leave. This was his chance to see the world.

7   Four months later, Lu Yang stepped off the boat in San Francisco into a different world. Familiar sights mixed with strange new sights. There were men everywhere shouting and waving their arms. Many of these men were Chinese, wearing the same neat tunic and pants as his, their black hair tied in long pigtails down their backs. But there were also large white men with hairy faces and dirty clothes. Noise from these men, as well as Chinese voices and the cries of the seabirds, filled Lu Yang's ears. For a minute he felt dizzy as his hunger and sickness from the terrible journey caught up with him. Then the feeling passed as a Chinese man approached him and spoke to him in words he understood. The man told Lu Yang and his cousin to follow, and they set off through the bustling crowd.

8   Once away from the ships, it was quieter and less confusing. Here there were more Chinese than white men. Some looked shocked and confused; others moved

---

[3] **emperor:** a ruler of a large country

continued

around confidently, organizing the newcomers. Lu Yang felt his cousin nudge him, and he looked to where Ah Min was staring. He saw a tall wooden platform that was the height of a man's shoulders. Five Chinese girls, eyes to the ground, were standing on the platform. They were wearing only light cotton underwear and their thin bodies were shivering in the cold. Chinese and white men were walking around the platform shouting and waving money in the air. As Lu Yang watched, a white man walked up the steps to the platform, handed another Chinese man a bundle of bills, and half carried, half dragged one of the girls away.

9   Lu Yang's guide saw the two cousins staring at this sight. He answered their questioning look.

10   "Their fathers sold them to that man on the platform, Johnny Wu. He sells them for the highest price. He's a rich man now. He's never gotten his hands dirty digging for gold. His gold is warm and soft." The man spat in disgust and shook his head. "If a woman is lucky and beautiful, a white man or a rich Chinese man will buy her for his wife. If she is not lucky, she will be the wife of any and every man with a dollar to spare."

11   "But their fathers believed . . ." said Lu Yang.

12   "It doesn't matter what their fathers believed," said the guide. "This is reality. Welcome to Gum Shan."

After You Read

How Well Did You Read?

_____ 1. This is a true story about a young Chinese immigrant to America.

_____ 2. Lu Yang's father was an herbalist, but he did not have enough money for his family.

_____ 3. Lu Yang thought he would be away from his family for two years.

_____ 4. Lu Yang was married.

Discussing the Reading

Work with a partner. Answer the questions about Reading 3. Use complete sentences.

1. The first few paragraphs show the reader that Lu Yang's family had a hard life. What details does the writer use to show us how difficult life was for this family? Write down five details. The first is done for you. Note that when we write about people in a story, we use the present tense.

   a. Lu Yang is very tired and very hungry.

   b. _____

   c. _____

   d. _____

   e. _____

2. What does Lu Yang see when he arrives in San Francisco? Write down four things.

   a. He sees a lot of Chinese men and some white men.

   b. _____

   c. _____

   d. _____

3. How do you think Lu Yang and his cousin feel when they arrive in San Francisco? Use *because* to give reasons for your answers.

   a. I think they feel frightened because San Francisco is different from their home.

   b. _____

   c. _____

   d. _____

Check Your Understanding

Circle the letter of the best answer.

1. What would be a good title for this story?

   a. Lu Yang and Ah Min's Journey to America
   b. From One World to Another
   c. Gold Discovered in California!

2. Which statement is correct according to the first paragraph?

   a. The family farmed two mus of land the year before the story begins.
   b. The family owned more than two mus of land the year before the story starts.
   c. The family grew crops on more than two mus of land the year before the story begins.

3. Why are the younger brothers building a dam?

   a. They don't want the topsoil to wash away down the hillside.
   b. They need to trap the water so they can have water in the summer.
   c. They are trying to stop the large stones from escaping down the hillside.

4. What is the main idea of paragraph 2?

   a. Ah Min visits the family and shares a meal with them.
   b. Ah Min tells the family about the gold discovery in America.
   c. Ah Min tells the family about the herbalist who came to his village.

5. Why can't Lu Yang get married that year?

   a. He doesn't know anyone he wants to marry.
   b. He has to work to help his family.
   c. His father doesn't have enough money for a bride-price.

6. Why does the family keep jars under the floor in their home?

   a. It is cold and dark under the floor.
   b. They hope robbers will not find the jars.
   c. Air will not pass through the jars under the floor.

7. Why do you think Lu Yang's father tells him "True gold is here in your home with your family and ancestors"?

   a. He wants Lu Yang to remember that gold will save the family.
   b. He is worried his son will forget that his family has gold.
   c. He wants Lu Yang to remember that his family is more important than gold.

8. Which statement is correct according to paragraph 7?

   a. Lu Yang was sick on the journey from China to San Francisco.
   b. Everything in San Francisco was strange to Lu Yang.
   c. Lu Yang had never seen Chinese men wearing blue tunics before.

9. Why does the guide say Johnny Wu's gold is "warm and soft?"

   a. Johnny Wu has a lot of gold and so he is very rich.
   b. Johnny Wu pays other men to get their hands dirty digging for gold.
   c. Johnny Wu gets his gold from selling women, not from digging for gold.

10. Why do you think the guide says, *"It doesn't matter what their fathers believed. This is reality. Welcome to Gum Shan."*

   a. He wants the two cousins to feel welcome in their new land.
   b. He is telling the cousins that life is difficult and not what they expected in this new land.
   c. He believes fathers are not important.

Vocabulary Skill

Understanding the Prefix dis-

A **prefix** is a letter or group of letters that is added to the beginning of a word. When a prefix is added, it changes the meaning of the word. In Reading 3, Lu Yang's mother *disagreed* with her husband's decision. *Agree* is the base word. The prefix *dis-* changes the base word to the opposite meaning. *Disagree* therefore means to have a different opinion from another person. Several words can have the opposite meaning with the prefix *dis-*:

agree with	disagree with	like	dislike
appear	disappear	obey	disobey
approve of	disapprove of	own	disown
connect	disconnect	trust	distrust

A. Work with a partner. Read the list of words above and talk about their meanings. If you are not sure about the meaning, use an English dictionary.

B. Complete each sentence with the best word from the list. Use the present or future tense. Make sure the verb agrees with its subject. In some cases, more than one answer is correct.

1. If you don't pay your telephone bill, the telephone company will
   _____ your phone. Then you won't be able to make any calls.

2. My parents _____ the way I am raising my children. They think I should have more rules and give the children less freedom.

3. I _____ my sixteen-year-old son having a part-time job. He needs to spend his time studying, not working. However, he wants to work because he wants to earn some money.

continued

4. In American culture, many people _____ you if you don't look them right in the eye. They think you are not telling the truth if you do not look at them.

5. There is a well-known expression: Money _____ like water. One minute you have it. The next minute it is gone!

6. My neighbors said they will _____ their son if he continues to get into trouble with the police. I hope they change their mind because I think the boy needs their help and I believe it is their job as parents to help him.

7. Soldiers who _____ orders can get into serious trouble. They are trained to do what they are told.

8. Many people _____ using animals to test scientific products. They think the testing hurts the animals and is therefore cruel. They believe scientists should not use animals for testing products.

C. Complete the sentences using your own words.

1. I disapprove of the way my friend behaves in class. She always _____

   _____.

2. You should disconnect your computer if _____.

3. I distrust my neighbor because he _____.

4. Some people dislike children who _____.

5. The students disagreed with their teacher. The teacher thought it was not a good idea to use dictionaries in class, but the students thought _____

   _____.

6. My father disowned my sister because she _____.

7. My family is very strict. If I disobey my parents, they will _____

   _____.

8. Every time I ask my son to do his homework, he disappears. He runs into ____

   _____.

Vocabulary Review

A. Choose the best word or words to complete each sentence.

confidently	ancestors	crisis	objectively
adapt	influence	conflict	criticizes
acceptable behavior	adolescence		

1. Mr. James is a good English teacher. He _____ my writing by pointing out my mistakes, but he also helps me fix those mistakes.

2. I don't like my daughter's boyfriend. I have tried to think about him _____, listing all the good things and all the bad things about him. I think there are more bad things than good, but my daughter does not agree with me.

3. I think family history is very interesting. I am trying to find out exactly where my _____ came from.

4. _____ is the bridge between being a child and being an adult.

5. Sticking your tongue out at your brother is not _____. You must be more polite to people.

6. If there is _____ between parents and their teenage children, everyone should try to compromise to make things better.

7. Juan had been in the country for six months and was suffering from culture shock. Things came to a _____ when he decided he hated living in this country and wanted to go home. Luckily, this was the worst stage, and he began to feel more comfortable living here.

8. Many people experience culture shock while they are trying to _____ to a new and different culture.

9. Lee plays the piano very _____ even though he's only twelve. He's been playing since he was three.

10. My friend has a very good _____ on me. When I get mad, she calms me down; if I'm lazy and I don't want to do my homework, she tells me I must do it. I'm lucky to have her as a friend.

B. **Complete the sentences using your own words.**

1. My parents are always _____ me. They think I am

   _____.

2. The tomato seeds will grow quickly if you _____.

3. Last night I felt dizzy because I _____.

4. The most important rule about driving is never _____.

5. The bank manager refused to give _____.

6. My son's friends are a bad influence because they _____.

7. _____ is not acceptable behavior in class.

8. There are many benefits to traveling. For example, you learn about _____

   _____.

9. It is important to try to adapt to a new culture. For example, you should

   _____.

10. I don't speak English confidently because _____.

Expanding the Topic

Connecting Reading with Writing

Choose one of the topics to write about.

1. Think of a time when you and your parents did not agree about something. Explain the problem clearly. What did you want to do? What did your parents want to do? What happened? Did you make a compromise and, if you did, what was that compromise? Write a paragraph that describes this situation and answers all of these questions.

2. Your teacher has asked you to interview several students of English to ask them about their experiences with culture shock. First of all, write down five questions to ask. Then interview two students. Ask them the questions, and make notes about their answers. Write a paragraph about their experiences.

3. You lived in Canada for two years while you were studying business at a college. You have now returned to Taiwan. Your best friend, Andrew, left Taiwan two months ago to study at the same college in Canada. He has written to you and told you he is feeling very unhappy. He hates everything about his new life and is thinking about leaving college and returning home to Taiwan. Write a letter to Andrew. Explain to him that you think he is suffering from culture shock. Tell him how you felt when you first arrived. Give him some advice about how to improve his life. Use information and vocabulary from the readings to make your letter interesting.

4. You have read the story about Lu Yang. What do you think happens to him in California? Do you think he finds gold? Is his life easy or difficult? Is he happy in his new life? Does he return to his home to help his family? Does he find a wife? Imagine you are the author who wrote this story. Write two or three paragraphs to finish the story. Use your imagination.

Exploring Online

Choose one of the following assignments.

1. Reading 1 in this chapter describes four stages of culture shock. Some people suffer from a fifth stage, which is known as reverse culture shock. Do an online search to find out more about reverse culture shock. Then write a paragraph explaining what it is and what you can do to help someone who is suffering from reverse culture shock. Remember to write down where your information comes from.

2. The story "Welcome to Gum Shan" is about a time in Californian history known as the Gold Rush. Do an online search to answer the following questions about this time:

   a. When did the Gold Rush begin?
   b. Who was the first person to find gold?
   c. How did people travel from the East Coast of America to California?
   d. How did people look for gold?
   e. How many people traveled to California during the first five years of the Gold Rush?

   Write down the name and address of the Web site where you found the answers to these questions. Share your answers with your class. Did you all get the same answers? Did you use the same Web sites?

3. Many Chinese men like Lu Yang left China to look for gold during the California Gold Rush. It was much more unusual for Chinese women to come to California during this time. However, a young woman called Lalu Nathoy left China for California. Do an online search to answer the following questions about Lalu Nathoy. Write in complete sentences.

   a. Why did Lalu leave her home?
   b. When did she arrive in California?
   c. What happened to her when she arrived in California?
   d. What did people call her in America?
   e. What jobs did she have when she lived in Idaho?
   f. Who did she marry?
   g. What is the name of the movie that is about Lalu's life?

   Write down the name of the Web site you used to answer these questions.

CHAPTER

Health Matters

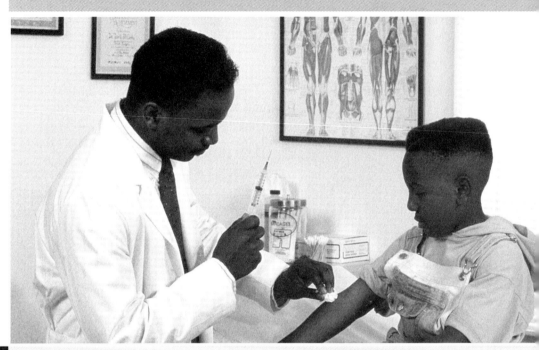

This chapter is about health. Reading 1 begins with a magazine article about a variety of health issues. Reading 2 is also a magazine article. It describes how to perform a lifesaving process. The third reading describes how the heart functions, or works, and what happens when the heart cannot function properly.

In this chapter, you will practice:

Reading Skills

➡ Previewing a reading

➡ Scanning for information

Vocabulary Skills

➡ Using context clues to understand vocabulary

➡ Previewing vocabulary

➡ Understanding phrasal verbs with *run*

Life Skills

➡ Explaining how to do something

➡ Finding basic medical information online

Before You Read

Work in small groups. Discuss the questions and complete the tasks.

1. Look at the illustrations. What's wrong with these people? Write a sentence below each person describing the problem. Make sure you know how to describe what is wrong with each person before you continue to the next questions.

a. _____

_____

b. _____

c. _____

d. _____

_____

e. _____

_____

continued

2. What do you do if you have a headache?
What do you do if your child/friend has a high fever?
What do you do if you have a stomachache, and you are vomiting?

3. You share an apartment with a friend. Your friend is sick. How do you decide if you need to call a doctor?

4. If you already have a family doctor, how did you find this doctor? If you don't have a doctor, what will you do if you need to see one?

5. Different people feel comfortable with different doctors. What kind of doctor do you prefer? Do you prefer a man or a woman, for example?

Using Context Clues to Understand Vocabulary

The words in bold print are in Reading 1. Guess the meaning of each word by looking at the context. Circle the letter of the best answer.

1. While I was skiing, I fell and twisted my ankle. My foot was so **swollen** I could not put my shoe on.

   a. painful
   b. seriously injured
   c. increased in size

2. I cut my finger last week at work. It wasn't a bad cut, and it didn't look dirty, so I didn't wash it very carefully. Two days later my whole hand hurt and was red. The doctor told me I had an **infection,** because I didn't clean the cut properly.

   a. fever
   b. illness caused by bacteria
   c. dirty cut

3. I was awake during the **surgery,** but I didn't watch as the doctors fixed my bad knee. Luckily, I never felt a thing. After they sewed me up, they told me I was fine.

   a. a medical procedure that involves cutting into the body
   b. an X-ray of a broken bone
   c. a very bad dream

4. There is no **cure** for AIDS, but modern medicine has improved the lives of AIDS patients. Doctors will continue to search for ways to make patients completely better.

   a. medicine that is needed for a serious illness
   b. medicine that takes away the pain in an illness
   c. medicine that makes an illness go away

5. I like to read "How to" books: *How to Fix Your Car, How to Cook Healthy Food, How to Install Computer Software.* I find it interesting to read about a **process** and then try to do it myself.

   a. a series of steps you take in order to complete an action
   b. an interesting book which teaches you how to do things
   c. a program on the computer

Now Read

THE ABC'S OF EVERYDAY HEALTH

***Health Weekly*'s**

New Series!!!

Today we begin a new series about what you need to know to keep healthy, fit, and safe . . . *The ABC's of Everyday Health.* Each week, we'll work through the alphabet to provide you with up-to-date information about health issues of today. We'll talk about definitions, symptoms, and possible treatments. This week, we begin with . . .

A: Asthma

Asthma is a serious condition that puts half a million Americans in the hospital each year. During an asthma attack, the main airways for the lungs, the bronchial tubes, become swollen and sore. The muscles around the bronchial tubes tighten, which produces a lot of mucus—sticky, thick liquid. This makes it very difficult to breathe. In severe attacks, the patient is unable to breathe and will need hospital care in order to survive the attack.

Anyone can get asthma at any age, although you are more likely to get this condition if your parents suffer from it or other breathing disorders. In other words, it is often hereditary. Allergies and environmental pollution can also trigger, or start, asthma. People who live in large cities with high levels of air pollution or those who work around people who smoke are more likely to suffer from asthma.

Like many conditions, symptoms can vary from person to person. Some asthma sufferers only have a very occasional attack, perhaps once every two or three years. During this attack, they experience shortness of breath as they try to breathe. They may also have a cough. Other sufferers have *chronic* asthma—they experience more frequent and serious attacks. The chest feels tight, and it quickly becomes more difficult to get enough air.

Most asthma sufferers need prescription medication. Anyone

continued

---

who thinks they may have experienced an asthma attack should therefore see a doctor immediately. However, you can do a few things to limit asthma attacks: Ask your doctor about exercises to strengthen your heart and lungs; keep your home clean; stay away from people who smoke.

B: Broken Bones

A broken bone is also called a fracture. It is a common injury, especially for children playing sports or just being children and falling out of trees! There are different types of fractures. A bone can break completely or partially. A compound fracture is a serious break because the bone breaks through the skin. Therefore, the additional problems of bleeding and infection may occur. However, all breaks are medical emergencies and require medical assistance.

Kids are always falling down and bruising themselves, so how do you know if your child has broken an arm or just bruised it? Sometimes the patient hears a snap or a crack as he or she falls. This is clear sign of a broken bone. The bone might also be broken if the person cannot move the arm without a lot of pain.

If you think someone has broken a bone, try not to move the injured part, and call for medical assistance immediately. While you are waiting for help, keep the person warm, but don't give him or her anything to drink or eat, in case the person requires surgery.

A doctor will usually X-ray the injured area. Sometimes, the doctor will need to reposition the broken bone. Then a cast is normally placed around the injured leg or arm to stop the bone from moving. The bone will then repair itself. This can take anywhere from several weeks to several months.

C: CPR

Cardiovascular disease—heart disease—is the leading cause of death for Americans. This disease killed 931,108 Americans in 2001, according to the American Heart Association (AHA). Most people suffer a heart attack at home and only have a 2–5% chance of recovery. Your chances of recovery increase, however, if someone gives you CPR (cardiopulmonary resuscitation) within five minutes of your collapse and calls 911. CPR is a lifesaver.

A person provides CPR by pressing down on the patient's chest repeatedly and breathing into the patient's mouth. This action keeps a small amount of oxygen flowing into the heart—without oxygen the heart will quickly die. CPR does not cure heart attack victims; it keeps people alive until medics arrive with advanced medical equipment.

The AHA believes every adult should know how to give CPR. It is a simple process. You take a class (4–8 hours), and the instructor teaches you what to do. Very importantly, during a class, you can

continued

practice giving CPR to a dummy (a life-size doll). You also learn the important differences between giving CPR to an adult and to a child. So take a class, and perhaps save a life.

D: Depression

Today, most people understand that depression is a mental illness. People who have depression feel very sad and hopeless. Doctors believe that people who suffer from this illness may have an imbalance in certain brain chemicals called *neurotransmitters*. They think this imbalance causes feelings of sadness. However, doctors say they need to study this disease a lot more before they really understand it.

There are several reasons why people become seriously depressed. Some doctors believe depression is hereditary, so you are more likely to become depressed if you have a family history of depression. Stress and serious illnesses can also trigger depression. Some prescription medications list depression as a side effect. Women sometimes suffer from depression after they have a baby. This is called *postpartum* depression.

People have different symptoms of depression. Most depressed people no longer enjoy day-to-day activities that they used to enjoy. They feel sad and hopeless and often cry a lot. Some are unable to sleep, but others may sleep too much. Most people feel tired all the time. Some people lose a lot of weight when they are depressed; others gain a lot of weight. If people were sexually active before they become depressed, they can lose their interest in sex. Depressed people have a very negative view of life and themselves. Thoughts about death are common. In extremely serious cases, depression can lead to suicide.

There is no simple explanation for depression, and there is no simple cure. Doctors treat depression in different ways. They usually suggest therapy. The patient meets with an expert therapist on a regular basis and talks about things that might be causing depression. Therapists help people understand their problems. Doctors also often prescribe medication. These medications work on correcting the imbalance of the neurotransmitters. Medication and therapy combined are often very successful in helping people live with this illness.

After You Read

How Well Did You Read?

Read the statements. Write *T* (true), *F* (false), or *N* (not enough information).

_____ **1.** Next week, the magazine will write about allergies, as part of this series.

_____ **2.** All asthma sufferers have frequent and very serious attacks.

_____ **3.** Sometimes a person can actually hear a bone break as he or she falls.

_____ **4.** Heart disease kills more men than women.

Reading Skill

Scanning for Information

We read for different purposes. Sometimes we need to read all of an article or chapter because we need to understand the main ideas. For example, if your teacher asks you to read a newspaper article and then write what you think about that article, you will need to read the whole article. Other times, however, we read to find a specific piece of information—a detail. For example, if you want to know what time the news starts on channel 4, you do not need to read the whole *TV Guide.* You quickly turn to the correct page and **scan,** or quickly look, for the information.

When you scan for details,

- decide what information you need.
- identify important, or key, words to help find this information.
- think about the key words, and quickly move your eyes down the page. Don't read; just scan for the key words.
- read the sentences around the key words to make sure you have found the correct information.

    Example:

Question:	According to Reading 1, what can trigger, or start, asthma?
Information needed:	*what triggers asthma*
Key words:	*trigger, asthma*
Answer:	Allergies and pollution

Read the questions. Underline the key words in each question. Then scan Reading 1 for the answers. You do not need to answer in complete sentences.

1. What happens during a chronic asthma attack?

   _____

2. How many Americans died from heart disease in 2001?

   _____

3. What is a compound fracture?

   _____

4. Why do doctors put a cast around a broken bone?

   _____

5. Give two reasons why people become depressed:

   _____

6. What is CPR?

   _____

7. What is the AHA?

   _____

8. What are neurotransmitters?

   _____

9. What do women sometimes suffer from after they have a baby?

   _____

10. What are two symptoms of depression?

   _____

Using Context Clues to Understand Vocabulary

These words are in Reading 1. Scan for each word in the reading, and read the sentences around it to understand the word. Then choose the best word to complete each sentence.

hereditary	dummy	mucus	assistance
frequent	negative	trigger	unable
occasional	chronic		

1. I get _____ headaches, but they are not very bad ones. I only get these headaches once or twice a year.

2. When I was a medical student, I practiced putting a cast on a _____. This was much better than using a real person!

3. The student asked the librarian for _____ because he couldn't find the book he needed.

4. When you have a bad cold, it is hard to breathe because of all the _____ in your nose.

5. Per was _____ to get up because he had broken his leg. He couldn't move.

6. Asthma can be _____. If your parents suffer from this illness, you may also get it at some time in your life.

7. Tony often misses class. His teacher is worried about his _____ absences.

8. My friend has _____ thoughts about her math class. She thinks she is going to fail because she doesn't understand math very well. She also thinks the teacher is boring and the textbook is confusing.

9. Breathing in someone else's smoke can _____ an asthma attack.

10. Unfortunately, depression can be a _____ illness that keeps coming back.

How to Give CPR

Before You Read

Previewing

Work with a partner. Discuss the questions.

1. Read the title, and look at the illustrations in Reading 2 on pages 173 and 174. What is this reading about?

2. Have you ever taken a CPR class? If so, what did you learn in this class?

3. What would you do if your teacher suddenly fell down in the classroom and stopped breathing?

Now Read

The magazine *Health Weekly* also has a "How to . . ." section each week. This tells readers how to do useful things to keep themselves and others healthy and safe.

HOW TO GIVE CPR

Health Weekly's **How to . . .**

Be Safe, Be Happy, Be Healthy

This Week: How to Give CPR

Readers: Please note that this article is only a guide to performing this life-saving process. The American Heart Association recommends that all adults take a CPR[1] class from a skilled instructor.

Imagine this: You are at home watching TV with your husband. He tells you he is not feeling well and is going to lie down. He stands up to leave the room but suddenly falls down. What do you do?

STEP 1: CALL 911

<u>Quickly</u> check the victim for unresponsiveness.

- Shout at him or her.
- Watch for movement.
- Watch for breathing.

[1] Guidelines for giving CPR, particularly mouth-to-mouth resuscitation, change from time to time. Always check with the American Heart Association or the Red Cross for up-to-date information.

continued

<u>Call 911</u>.

- Tell the emergency dispatcher "This is an emergency."
- Tell the dispatcher the victim is unresponsive: "My husband is unresponsive."
- Give your address.
- Follow the directions of the emergency dispatcher. The dispatcher may ask you to begin CPR.
- Before you begin CPR, unlock your front door if necessary.

STEP 2: BLOW

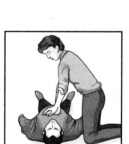

- Make sure the victim is lying on the floor, on his or her back.
- Tilt the head back, and look inside the mouth for anything blocking the airway.
- Listen and watch for breathing.
- If there is no breathing, close the victim's nostrils with your fingers.
- Cover his or her mouth with yours and give two breaths.
- As you breathe, watch for the chest to rise.

STEP 3: PRESS

- After two breaths, check if the victim is breathing.
- If there is no breathing, place your hands on the center of the chest.
- Put one hand on top of the other.
- Push down on the victim's chest 15 times at the rate of 100/minute.
- Press down 1 to 2 inches.

STEP 4: REPEAT

- Repeat steps 2 and 3 until help arrives.

After You Read

How Well Did You Read?

Read the statements. Write *T* (true), *F* (false), or *N* (not enough information).

_____ **1.** Call 911 as soon as you see a person is unconscious.

_____ **2.** Unlock the front door before the medical assistance arrives.

_____ **3.** Breathe twice into the victim's nose.

_____ **4.** Begin CPR before you call 911.

Life Skill

Explaining How to Do Something

When you explain how to do something, you provide a series of steps or instructions. This is called a **process.** When we write about a process, we

- often use the imperative form of the verb.
- only write about important information.
- make sure the steps are in the correct order.

Example:

Call 911 as quickly as possible.

Move the head back and listen for breathing.

The **imperative** is the base form of the verb. The subject of the sentence is *you*, but this is not written in the sentence. The imperative form is the same in singular and plural.

Example:

<u>John</u>, sit down right now. (singular subject)

<u>Mary and Augustus</u>, be quiet. (plural subject)

We use the imperative to give instructions, orders, advice, and warnings. We make a negative imperative statement by adding *do not, don't,* or *never* before the verb.

Read the following paragraphs. Each paragraph explains how to do something. However, the writer has not used the imperative, has not put the steps in the correct order, and has included unnecessary information. Therefore it is difficult to clearly follow these instructions. Rewrite each paragraph into a clear set of instructions. Use the imperative and make sure the steps are correctly organized.

1. How to Warm Up Before Exercising

   It is really important to warm up before you start your exercise. Even people who exercise frequently should always warm up. I do, and I exercise once a day. There are different ways to warm up, but this is what I do. The first thing I do is move my neck forward and backward. This relaxes the muscles. It feels really good. Then I move my neck from side to side. I also like to stretch my back. I stand with my legs slightly apart, my hands on my hips, and I bend from one side to another. Before I work on my back, I stand against a wall and lean forward with my back leg straight and my front leg bent. This stretches my calves. Then I am ready for my morning jog. Of course, before you do any of this, you must wear sensible clothing—cotton is best. Make sure you have strong, well-fitting running shoes.

   How to Warm Up Before Exercising

   <u>Move your neck forward and backward.</u>

   _____

   _____

   _____

   _____

   _____

2. How to Get the Most Out of Walking

   Marie walks every day, and at the end of her walk, she cools down by doing some stretching exercises. She is very careful to warm up properly first. She doesn't need to lose weight; she just wants to be healthy. She often walks through the park, although on weekends, she goes to the neighborhood school and walks around the football field. She knows how to get the most out of her walks. She wears good walking shoes and light clothing. After warming up, she starts walking quite slowly for the first ten minutes. Then she gradually increases her speed. She carries a pedometer[1] with her to check her speed. After 30 minutes of fast walking, Mary slows down for the last 10 minutes. She never puts her hands in her pockets or holds them straight. Instead, she bends her arms at the elbows and moves them back and forth as she walks. Finally, she

[1] **pedometer:** a small instrument that measures how far you walk

takes short walking strides—not long ones. She places her heel on the ground first and then rolls to her toe. You should not put your foot down flat.

How to Get the Most Out of Walking

_____

_____

_____

_____

_____

Reading 3 | *The Amazing Human Heart*

Before You Read

How much do you know about your heart? Take this quiz to see how much you know. If you don't know the answers scan Reading 3 to find the information. Remember to look for key words as you scan.

1. How big is the adult heart?

   a. the size of your foot
   b. the size of your open hand
   c. the size of a clenched fist

2. How many times does the heart beat every day?

   a. 100 times
   b. 100,000 times
   c. 1,000,000 times

3. How many miles does your blood travel through your body each day?

   a. 6 miles
   b. 600 miles
   c. 60,000 miles

4. What causes the *bu–bump* noise your heart makes?

   a. love
   b. the heart valves opening and shutting
   c. your lungs bumping against your heart

5. Where is your heart?

   a. roughly in the center of your chest
   b. completely on the left side of your chest
   c. completely on the right side of your chest

Previewing Vocabulary

These words are in Reading 3. Read the words and their definitions. Then choose the best word to complete each sentence.

Word	Definition
efficient	working well, doing something quickly and without wasting time
extremely	very
flows	moves in a steady stream
immediate	happening at once, without delay
lungs	organs of the body used for breathing
organ	a part of the body that has a special purpose, like the heart or the lungs
pump	a machine that forces liquid or gas into or out of something
valve	a part of a tube or pipe that opens and closes like a door in order to control the flow of liquid or gas passing through

1. Some drivers on German freeways drive _____ fast. They drive over 100 mph.

2. When the teacher saw the boy fall down and cut his head, she called for _____ help.

3. The _____ wasn't working at the gas station. I couldn't get any gas.

4. Smoking can seriously damage your _____.

5. If you are an _____ donor, it means that doctors can use parts of your body after you die to help somebody else.

6. The new manager is very _____. She is very organized, and she works very hard.

7. The Columbia River _____ into the Pacific Ocean.

8. A bicycle pump has a _____ that lets air go through it, but stops the air from returning.

Now Read

The Amazing Human Heart

1   For thousands of years, people have believed that the heart controls feelings, particularly love. The heart shape is a symbol of love, and Cupid[1] aims his arrow at the heart to make a person fall in love. We talk about a broken heart if someone is unlucky in love. If someone is mean, we call him or her "cold-hearted" or "hard-hearted." If someone is a really good person, we say he or she is "big-hearted" or that they have a heart of gold. In reality, however, the heart has nothing to do with love or other feelings.

2   For a start, the heart does not look like the neat red heart on a valentine. It is much more complicated than that simple shape. It is as big as a clenched fist, and it lies roughly in the middle of the chest—not completely to the left, as people often believe. It has four chambers, or main parts. The top two chambers are called the atria. The bottom two chambers are called the ventricles. Arteries and veins lead in and out of these chambers. The arteries and veins carry the blood to and from the heart. The whole organ is protected by a special muscle called the myocardium.

3   The heart is responsible for pumping blood around the body. Blood carries oxygen; without oxygen, a human body can only live for a few minutes. Each part of the heart has its own job. Blood flows from a vein called the superior vena cava into the right atrium (singular form of *atria*). This blood has already traveled around the body, so it is low in oxygen. When blood is low in oxygen, it is a bluish color. This blood passes through the tricuspid valve into the right ventricle. As the valve opens and shuts, it makes the *bu-bump* heart noise. The powerful ventricle then pumps the blood through the pulmonary valve into the pulmonary artery, which leads to the lungs. Here the blood fills up on oxygen from the air the lungs breathe in.

4   Now the blood is bright red and rich in oxygen. It flows back to the heart and into the left atrium. It moves through the bicuspid valve to the left ventricle. The powerful ventricle then pumps the blood through the aortic valve into the aortic artery. It flows through this artery to the rest of the body, providing oxygen to every single cell in the body. Once the blood has run out of oxygen, the superior vena cava returns the blood to the right atrium to begin the process over again.

5   A normal heart beats 60–100 times a minute. This is 100,000 times a day and over two billion times in a lifetime. As it beats, the heart pumps blood through 60,000 miles of arteries, veins, and capillaries, which make up the blood vessels.

[1] **Cupid:** The Roman god of love, who carries a bow and arrow

continued

Arteries carry oxygen-rich blood to the rest of the body; veins carry oxygen-poor blood back to the heart and lungs to be refilled with oxygen. The heart, lungs, and blood vessels make up the circulatory system.

6   The heart is an extremely strong, efficient organ if we look after it. However, like any complicated machine, there are many things that can go wrong with it, especially if we do not look after it properly. A common type of heart disease is arteriosclerosis. This disease affects the arteries that carry the oxygen. It can happen when people have high cholesterol. Cholesterol is a natural part of the blood, but it needs to be at the right level. If a person has too much bad cholesterol (LDL) and too little good cholesterol (HDL), then parts of the cholesterol break off and stick to the inside of the arteries. These bits are called deposits. As more deposits stick, the artery walls become hard and thick. There is less room for the blood to flow. Therefore the heart has to work harder to keep pushing the blood through the arteries. If the deposits completely block an artery, the blood cannot get through. This can result in a heart attack and the victim will need immediate CPR and medical assistance to stay alive.

7   The heart may not be responsible for love, but without it, we won't be around to fall in love! So look after it. Follow the guidelines from the American Heart Association: Don't smoke, eat healthy food, and exercise regularly. You want this amazing machine to be pumping for you for a long time.

After You Read

How Well Did You Read?

Read the statements. Write *T* (true), *F* (false), or *N* (not enough information).

_____ 1. The heart controls feelings.

_____ 2. The heart acts as a pump.

_____ 3. Arteries and veins carry oxygen-rich blood to the body.

_____ 4. The hardening of arteries is a symptom of arteriosclerosis.

Check Your Understanding

A. How the heart works is a complicated process. It often helps to understand this process by looking at a drawing, or diagram, as well as reading the text. Look at the following diagram. Note that in the diagram, the right side of the heart is on your left, and the left side of the heart is on your right. Use the information from Reading 3 to label the diagram correctly. One is completed for you.

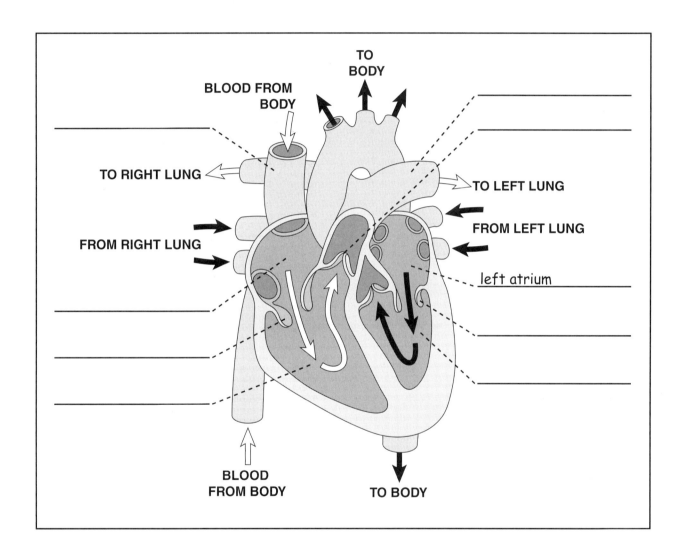

B. Look at these diagrams of an artery. Using information from the reading, explain what is happening in each diagram.

Diagram 1

_____

_____

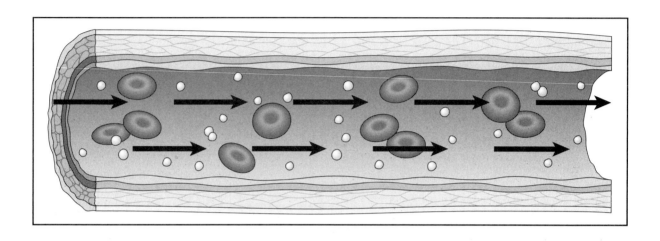

Diagram 2

_____

_____

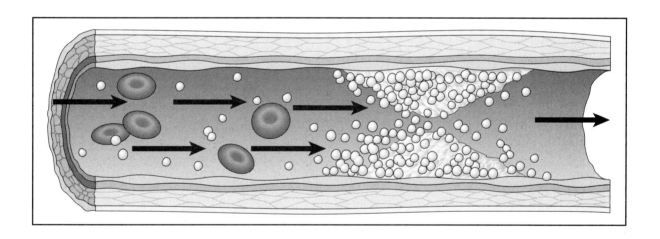

C. Circle the letter of the best answer.

1. *For thousands of years, people have believed that the heart controls feelings, particularly love.*

   This sentence means that

   a. people used to believe the heart controls love, but they don't believe this today.
   b. in the past, people believed the heart controls love. They still believe this today.
   c. these days, people believe the heart controls love.

2. *For a start, the heart does not look like the neat red heart on a valentine.* **It is much more complicated than that simple shape.**

   It stands for

   a. the heart.
   b. the simple shape.
   c. the valentine.

3. What is the main idea of paragraph 2?

   a. The heart has four chambers.
   b. The heart is protected by a special muscle.
   c. The heart has a complicated shape.

4. Which statement is correct according to the reading?

   a. Blood flowing into the right atrium is rich in oxygen.
   b. Veins carry blood that is full of oxygen.
   c. Oxygen-rich blood flows into the left atrium.

5. What is the purpose of the ventricles?

   a. They pump the blood on to the next part of its journey.
   b. They carry the blood to the heart.
   c. They carry the blood to the lungs to be filled up with oxygen.

6. What is the main idea of paragraphs 3 and 4?

   a. Blood carries oxygen, which the human body needs to live.
   b. The heart is responsible for pumping blood around the body.
   c. Blood flows to the lungs to fill up with oxygen.

7. What is the connection between the heart and the lungs?

   a. The lungs protect both sides of the heart.
   b. The lungs provide oxygen to the heart.
   c. The lungs provide oxygen to the blood that travels to the heart.

continued

8. *This disease affects the arteries that carry the oxygen. **It** can happen when people have high cholesterol.*

   It stands for

   a. oxygen.
   b. this disease.
   c. cholesterol.

9. Which statement is correct according to the reading?

   a. Cholesterol is good for arteries.
   b. HDL cholesterol is the bad kind of cholesterol.
   c. Cholesterol is a natural part of the body.

10. *As more deposits stick, the artery walls become hard and thick.*

    This sentence means that

    a. the artery walls should be soft and thin if they are healthy.
    b. before the deposits stick, the artery walls are hard and thick.
    c. the artery walls are blocked because of deposits.

Vocabulary Skill

Understanding Phrasal Verbs with Run

Reading 3 uses the phrasal verb *run out of.* This means to use all of something so there is nothing left. Here are some more phrasal verbs using *run:*

run across	meet someone by chance
run away	leave a place in order to escape from something or someone
run off (something)	quickly make some copies of something
run over	drive a car over something or someone
run through (something)	read, check, or explain something quickly
run up (something)	have to pay a big bill for something

A. Choose the best phrasal verb to complete each sentence. Use the past tense.

1. My daughter is always talking on her cell phone to her friends. Last month she _____ a huge phone bill.

2. The student felt very frustrated. He had spent a long time on his homework, but his printer _____ ink, and he couldn't print it.

3. I was nervous before the meeting with my boss. I _____ my ideas one more time with my co-worker before I went into the meeting.

4. I couldn't believe it! While I was traveling in Brazil, I _____ an old friend from college.

5. My neighbor _____ from her husband because he was violent. She went to a shelter for domestic violence victims.

6. My son left his bike behind my car. I _____ it when I backed out of the garage. Now he thinks I'm going to buy him a new bike.

7. I was late for an appointment, so my co-worker _____ fifty copies of the newsletter for me.

B. Now complete the sentences using your own words.

1. While I was on the freeway, I ran out of gas, so I _____.

2. Last night at the grocery store, my husband ran across _____.

3. I've run up a _____.

4. The girl ran away from school because _____.

5. Please run off _____.

6. My friend ran over his wife's _____.

7. Do you have a few minutes to run through _____?

Vocabulary Review

A. Choose the best word or words to complete each sentence.

infection	assistance	surgery	chronic
hereditary	flows	frequent	triggers
run out of	run up		

1. Some people say that chocolate _____ headaches.

2. My red hair is definitely _____. When my daughter was born, she had bright red hair, too.

3. If you don't wash a cut carefully, you may get a bad _____.

4. Blood _____ from the heart to the lungs to fill up with oxygen.

5. During the rainy season in Hong Kong, there are _____ storms. In fact, sometimes it seems as if it will never stop raining.

continued

6. The bank clerk couldn't answer my question, so he called his manager for
   _____.

7. It's easy to _____ huge bills with a credit card.

8. The mother called 911 because her son has _____ asthma
   and was having a serious attack. He could hardly breathe.

9. When my dog was hit by a car, it needed _____ to fix a
   badly broken leg.

10. I've _____ eggs. Could I borrow two?

B. Complete the sentences using your own words.

1. Although doctors cannot cure the common cold, _____.

2. My finger is swollen because I _____.

3. The organ donor sign on my driver's license means _____.

4. The teacher was unable to speak because she _____.

5. Occasional exercise will not _____.

6. Last week I ran across _____.

7. The traffic was moving extremely slowly because _____.

8. The student was very efficient and _____.

9. The police officer called for immediate help because _____.

10. If you want healthy lungs, you should _____.

Expanding the Topic

Connecting Reading with Writing

Choose one of the following writing assignments. Use ideas, information, and
vocabulary from the chapter to make your writing interesting.

1. Reading 1 began a new ABC series in a magazine about health issues. Each
   week, this magazine is going to present several different health issues as it works
   through the alphabet. Choose three letters of the alphabet. Think of an illness
   that begins with each letter. Write about each illness. Make sure you describe the
   symptoms and explain what the illness is and how a doctor treats it.

2. Reading 2 is about how to give CPR. Giving CPR is an example of a process.
   Think of something you know how to do. It does not have to be about
   medicine or health. For example, perhaps you know how to change a flat tire

on a car or how to set up a free e-mail system on your computer. Write a list of steps that describe how to do what you have chosen to describe. Make sure your steps are in the correct order and that you use the imperative.

3. The last reading in this chapter explains how the circulatory system works. Choose either the respiratory (breathing) system or the digestive (eating and drinking) system. Find a book in your library that has good diagrams of these systems. Draw one of the diagrams, and label it with the most important details. Write a short paragraph describing how the system works.

Exploring Online

Choose one or two of the following topics. Go online to answer the questions and complete the tasks.

1. A migraine is a serious headache. What are the symptoms of a migraine? What should you do if you get a migraine?

2. Your doctor has told you that you have high cholesterol and that you need to lose weight. Find two recipes for healthy food. Bring the recipes to class to share.

3. You want to take a CPR class. What is the closest class to you? When and where is it? How much does it cost?

4. You have never exercised before, and you have decided it is time to start. Find two or three exercises that are good for beginners. Print out these exercises, and bring them to class to share.

5. You are doing an online search to find information about how to warm up properly before exercising. First, type in the following as your search words: *warm up before exercising*. Next, type in *"warm up before exercising."* What happens when you put quotation marks around your search words?

Learning to Learn

CHAPTER

8

In this chapter you will read about some different aspects of education. Reading 1 is about test anxiety, which most students experience at some time in their educational career. Reading 2 describes how memory works and explains how to improve your memory. The last reading is a short story for you to enjoy. The story points out how the combination of making good decisions and getting a good education can change lives.

In this chapter, you will practice:

Reading Skills
→ Previewing a reading
→ Understanding main ideas
→ Reading between the lines

Vocabulary Skills
→ Using context clues to understand vocabulary
→ Previewing vocabulary
→ Choosing the correct word form

Life Skills
→ Setting realistic goals

188

How to Reduce Test Anxiety

Before You Read

Previewing

Work in small groups. Discuss the questions.

1. How do you prepare for a big test? Do you stay up late at night trying to study?

2. How do you feel the morning before a test?

3. How do you feel as you turn over the question sheet and begin to answer the questions?

4. How do you feel after the test?

Using Context Clues to Understand Vocabulary

The words in bold print are in Reading 1. Guess the meaning of each word by looking at the context. Circle the letter of the best answer.

1. When the body is very hot, it produces a liquid that forms on the skin. **Sweating** cools the skin and therefore cools the person. If you are perspiring a lot, it is important to drink a lot of water to replace the liquid the body is losing.

    a. exercising
    b. drinking water
    c. perspiring

2. Some people suffer from an **abnormal** fear of spiders. They cannot even look at a spider without feeling very frightened.

    a. common
    b. unusual
    c. stupid

3. Last night I was really embarrassed. I met an old friend at a party, but when I introduced her to my husband, I suddenly **went blank.** I just couldn't remember her name.

    a. was unable to remember anything
    b. felt dizzy
    c. felt very embarrassed

4. **Focusing** on your illness is not a good thing. Instead, you should try to think about getting better and how you will feel then.

    a. getting medical treatment
    b. thinking hard about something
    c. talking about

continued

5. If you find someone who is unconscious, it is **vital** that you call 911 and, if necessary, begin CPR. If you don't do this, the person may die.

    a. a little bit important
    b. extremely important
    c. a good idea

6. "You look really tired!"

    "I am. I forgot about the math test today, so I spent all last night **cramming** for it. Now I'm so tired, I can't remember anything I learned."

    a. studying in a sensible way
    b. worrying about something such as a test
    c. learning a lot of information fast

7. The English teacher asked the class to write a story about their lives. He told them to organize their writing **chronologically,** beginning with their first memory as a child and ending at the present time.

    a. neatly and correctly
    b. organized into paragraphs
    c. arranged according to when something happened

8. When I asked my son to think about some **realistic goals,** he told me he had a goal: He was going to work hard to try to win the lottery. I explained that this was not a realistic goal. Instead, I asked him to think about improving his grades at school and keeping his room tidy.

    a. something you want to do and can do in the future
    b. something that is impossible to do in the future
    c. something that will help your parents in the future

Now Read

How to Reduce Test Anxiety

1   Most teachers agree that it is normal to feel some nervousness or tension before a test. In fact, you usually perform better when you are a little nervous, because you try harder. So feeling nervous is a healthy and natural part of test taking. However, it is not healthy to feel so nervous that you go blank when you read the questions. It is also not normal to feel physically ill—to worry so much that you feel sick or dizzy. If you are this nervous, you are suffering from test anxiety.

2   How do you know whether you are suffering from normal nervousness or test anxiety? People experience different symptoms. Specific physical symptoms of test anxiety include:

continued

- sweating
- having headaches
- feeling sick
- feeling dizzy
- having an abnormal heartbeat

Mental or emotional symptoms of test anxiety include:

- going blank
- feeling stupid and worthless
- reading without understanding
- worrying that everyone else is better than you
- focusing on failing, not on passing

3   We can divide test anxiety into two kinds: normal and abnormal. If you have not prepared for the test properly, and you don't know or don't understand the material, it is completely normal to feel test anxiety. In other words, if you haven't studied well and don't know any of the answers, it is normal to feel physically ill. If, however, you have studied well throughout the class and you have prepared carefully for the test, but you still suffer symptoms of test anxiety, then this is not normal. You need to learn to overcome these feelings so that you can show the teacher exactly how much you have learned. In both situations, there are some simple steps that will help you overcome this anxiety and do better in tests.

4   Preparation is vital in test taking. It does not start the night before a test, however. Cramming at the last minute and staying up all night before the test is never the best way to study. You should prepare by taking good notes throughout the class and keeping those notes neatly in a chronologically organized binder. You must also keep up with your work and, very importantly, make an appointment to see the teacher if you don't understand something. Good students meet with their teachers for help once or twice throughout the course. The teachers usually have helpful suggestions about improving understanding. As the test date gets nearer, make a plan of what you need to review, or look over again. Try to predict what will be on the test and add this to your plan. Show your plan to your teacher to see if you are on the right track.

continued

5   Another important part of preparation is setting realistic goals. In most schools, grades are very important. It is normal to worry about your grade and to want a high grade. However, some students want to get 100% on every test and in every subject, and they feel depressed if they get a lower score. They put an enormous amount of pressure on themselves to be perfect, and most of us cannot be perfect all the time in every subject. So be realistic. Try to do the best you can, but don't always try to be perfect.

6   All students learn better and will suffer less anxiety if they set realistic goals and learn as they go. Research also shows that learners remember and understand information better and for longer periods of time if they write the information down instead of just trying to remember it. Preparing for a test is a skill, and you can easily learn how to do it well. Then, when that test comes along, you will be able to show the teacher how much you have learned rather than how nervous you are.

After You Read

How Well Did You Read?

Read the statements. Write *T* (true), *F* (false), or *N* (not enough information).

_____ **1.** It is normal to feel nervous before a test.

_____ **2.** Everyone suffering from test anxiety feels dizzy and goes blank.

_____ **3.** You can learn how to reduce test anxiety.

_____ **4.** Trying to get 100% on every test is an unrealistic goal.

Discussing the Reading

Work in small groups. Talk about the questions.

1. Paragraph 1 says that it is helpful to feel a little nervous in a test. Do you agree?

2. Do you experience any of the physical or mental symptoms mentioned in paragraph 2? What do you do during a test if you feel sick or go blank?

3. This reading says that cramming all night before a test is not a good idea. Do you agree? Have you ever crammed the night before a test? If so, did you pass the test?

4. This reading is in the last chapter of this book. You will probably have an end-of-course test soon. How are you preparing for that test? Do you know what kind of test you will have? Have you begun to study? Are you planning to cram the night before?

Check Your Understanding

Circle the letter of the best answer.

1. What is the main idea of the first paragraph?

   a. Although it is normal to feel a little nervous before a test, it is not normal to experience test anxiety if you have prepared well.
   b. Feeling nervous is a healthy and natural part of test taking.
   c. If you are very nervous, you are suffering from depression.

2. Which symptom of test anxiety is this student suffering from?

   "When I am taking a test, I look around and see that all my friends are writing very quickly. I'm just not as good as they are."

   a. going blank
   b. feeling dizzy
   c. worrying that everyone else is better than you

3. Which symptom of test anxiety is this person suffering from?

   "If I don't pass this class, my parents will be so mad. Maybe I can tell them I am really sick."

   a. feeling stupid and worthless
   b. focusing on failing, not on passing
   c. feeling sick

4. Which is an example of abnormal test anxiety according to this reading?

   a. "My mind went blank, even though I stayed up all night studying for this test."
   b. "I started sweating and feeling dizzy. All the weeks of preparation disappeared, and my mind went blank."
   c. "My heart started beating fast, and I felt very sick when I saw that the test was about a book I'd forgotten to read."

5. How is paragraph 4 organized?

   a. It compares different ways of preparing for a test.
   b. It describes a series of steps in a process.
   c. It contrasts different ways of preparing for a test.

6. Some students feel depressed if they get 85% in a test because _____

   a. this is a very low grade.
   b. this is a good grade.
   c. they have unrealistic goals.

7. What would be an example of a realistic goal for most people?

   a. "I want to travel around the world by the time I am thirty."
   b. "I want to have a part-time job that will give me good experience while I'm at college."
   c. "I want to get A's in every subject this year at college."

continued

8. What is the opposite of cramming according to the last paragraph?

   a. learning as you go
   b. setting realistic goals
   c. understanding how you learn

Choosing the Correct Word Form

A. Work with a partner. Read the words aloud. Reading 1 uses one or more forms of these words. Quickly scan the reading to find and underline the words. Talk about their meaning.

Verbs	Nouns	Adjectives
1.	anxiety	anxious
2. feel	feeling	
3. prepare	preparation	
4. study	student	studious
5. organize	organization	organized
6. suggest	suggestion	
7. inform	information	informative
8. perform	performance	

B. Choose the best word form to complete each sentence. When you use a verb, use the correct tense and make the verb agree with its subject. The number in the table above corresponds to the question number.

1. The student felt very _____anxious_____ before the test. Her _____anxiety_____ was so bad she felt dizzy and sick.

2. "Don't you have any _____ for me?" the actor cried.

   "Yes," replied the actress quietly. "I _____ sorry for you."

3. I didn't know about the test, so I didn't _____ for it. My lack of_____ earned me a failing grade.

4. My friend is very _____. Every night he _____ for two hours before dinner.

5. Juan's binder wasn't _____ at all. His papers were all over the place and he couldn't find anything. He decided to _____ his binder during lunch break.

6. "What can we do today?" asked Peter.

"Let's go to the movies," his friend _____.

"I have a better _____. Let's stay home and rent a movie."

7. There is a lot of good _____ about learning English on the Web. Our college, for example, has a very _____ Web site.

8. Most people _____ better on a test if they have had a good night's sleep. If they are tired, their _____ can suffer.

C. Complete the sentences using your own words.

1. It was after midnight and I was anxious because _____.

2. "How do you feel today?" asked the doctor.

"I have a _____."

3. Preparation is very important if _____.

4. I didn't prepare for the test, so last night I studied _____.

5. I must organize my _____.

6. The student had a good suggestion: "Let's_____."

7. I am so excited! My teacher has just informed me _____.

8. Sam's performance in class was not very good. He often _____

_____.

Setting Realistic Goals

Reading 1 talks about the importance of setting realistic goals. We can divide goals into short-term and long-term goals. *Short-term* means you want to achieve the goal quickly—perhaps within the next six months. *Long-term* means you will work for a long time before you achieve the goal.

When you decide on a realistic goal, you should think about the following:

- What do I want to achieve? Is this goal realistic?
- What problems make it difficult for me to achieve this goal?
- How will I overcome these problems? What steps will I take to achieve my goal?

Example:

Goal: I will learn to speak English more clearly, so I can talk to native speakers more comfortably. This is a realistic goal.

Problems: I don't know any native speakers, so it's hard for me to practice speaking English. I am shy and feel nervous when I talk. Other people don't understand my accent. I don't have a very good vocabulary.

Plan: I will read 10 pages every night to improve my vocabulary. I will listen to books on tape to improve my pronunciation. I will practice reading aloud. I will say one thing to my neighbor every day.

A. Work with a partner. Read these short-term goals. Each goal needs to be more realistic. Change the goal to make it more realistic.

Short-Term Goal	Problems	Plan
1. Peter has a part-time job and is studying engineering at college. His goal is to save enough money to buy a new car in two months.		
2. Jeanette wants to improve her grades. She's not very good at studying because she always leaves everything to the last minute and then tries to cram before a test. Her goal is to get 100% on her final test.		
3. Alicia is a single mother with a two-year-old daughter. Her goal is to get a full-time job as an office manager. She has never worked before.		

B. When you have made the goals more realistic, discuss with your partner problems that could make it difficult for these people to achieve their goals. Make a list of these problems in the space provided. Write in complete sentences.

C. Now work by yourself. Write a plan to help the people overcome the problems and achieve their goals. Make sure you address each problem.

D. Think of a short-term goal you want to achieve within the next six months. Discuss this goal with a partner. Make sure it is realistic. Talk about the problems and what you can do to overcome them. Complete this chart to clearly show how you can achieve your goal.

My Short-Term Goal	Problems	Plan

How Does Memory Work?

Before You Read

Previewing

Work in small groups. Discuss the questions and complete the tasks.

1. Look at the title and read the first sentence of each paragraph. What do you think this reading is going to be about?

2. Think for a minute about the subject of memory. Think of one question about memory you hope this reading will address. Write down this question.

   _____

3. Try this activity: Look at this series of numbers for three minutes. Then close the book. Write down as many of the numbers as you can remember. They must be in the correct order. Compare your memory with that of others in your group.

   4   12   7   3   2   8   19   5

4. How did you try to remember these numbers? How did the other students try to remember them?

5. Now here are the same numbers arranged like a telephone number. Look at this number for two minutes. Close the book. Write down the telephone number. Was it easier or more difficult to remember the numbers this time? Why?

   (425) 273-9181

6. When you learn English, you have to learn a lot of vocabulary. How do you remember new words? How do other members of your group learn new words?

Using Context Clues to Understand Vocabulary

The words in bold print are in Reading 2. Guess the meaning of each word by looking at the context. Circle the letter of the best answer.

1. I have two accounts at the bank: a checking account and a savings account. Last week I didn't have enough money in my checking account, so I **transferred** $30.00 from savings to checking.

   a. moved from one place to another
   b. saved money in an account
   c. paid a bill

continued

2. "Are you **familiar** with how the library is organized? Have you been to the library before?"

   a. not sure about something
   b. know something because you have experienced it at an earlier time
   c. feel confused about something

3. Reading is closely **connected** to writing. If you have problems reading, you will also have problems writing.

   a. having a relationship with something else
   b. being the opposite of something else
   c. being more difficult than something else

4. **Imagine** you are living in 2200. How will you get around from one place to another then?

   a. make a goal for the future
   b. think about something that is not real
   c. plan your life

5. Children are **dependent** on their parents when they are born: They cannot live without the care of their parents.

   a. very important
   b. weak, without power
   c. needing someone or something in order to exist

Now Read

How Does Memory Work?

1   "I'm studying Spanish, and I have a problem. I understand when the teacher is talking. She explains a new grammar point, and I understand. She gives us new words to learn, and I can remember them. The problem is, the next day I've forgotten what the grammar means, and I just can't remember the words. How can I ever learn when I can't remember?"

2   Does this sound familiar? Most of us have felt like this at some time in our lives. Certainly, students can get really frustrated if they can't remember information. As the student in the first paragraph asks, how can you learn if you don't remember? Luckily, you can learn how to improve your memory, and this, of course, helps you learn. In order to do this, you first need to understand how memory works. Like many other working machines, the brain follows a series of steps.

3   There is too much information in the world to remember everything. Therefore, you choose what you want to remember. Choosing is the first part of this

continued

process. If you are in a class for the first time, for example, you don't try to remember every student's name—there are too many. Instead, you choose to remember the name of the person sitting next to you.

4   The next part of the process is called encoding. *Encoding* means turning the information into a mental code that your memory can store. There are different ways to encode the information. You can encode something visually. Take the example in the previous paragraph. You are in class for the first time, and a student called Young-Hee is sitting next to you. You want to remember her name. Write it down. Remember what she looks like. You can also encode something by using sound. Ask Young-Hee how to pronounce her name, and listen carefully as she says it. Later, say her name aloud a few times. Another way of encoding is by thinking about the information and connecting it to something you already know. For example, you have another friend with the same name. Most memory experts agree that if you encode information in several ways, you will remember it more easily.

5   The third part of the memory process is storing the information. There are two ways our brain stores information. First, information moves into short-term memory. This part of memory can only keep a small piece of information for a short period of time. Imagine you ask a friend for a phone number. She gives you the phone number, you repeat it a couple of times to encode it, and then you dial the number. When you finish the call, you have forgotten the number. This is perfectly normal because the information, in this case a telephone number, was only in short-term memory.

6   It is very important to transfer some information from short-term memory to long-term memory. In the opening paragraph, the student is frustrated because she has encoded the information into her short-term memory but has not transferred it to her long-term memory. Therefore, she has forgotten it very quickly. Long-term memory is the part of the brain that can store a huge amount of information. So how do you transfer information from short-term to long-term memory?

7   You transfer information by repeating it and thinking about it. This is the time when remembering and understanding information are closely connected. Thinking about an important piece of information and repeating this information in your mind will help you understand it as well as remember it.

8   The final stage is finding the piece of information you have stored in your long-term memory. We call this retrieval, and this is the remembering part of the process. We find, or retrieve, things in different ways, just as we encode things in different ways. We can retrieve a piece of information by thinking of a visual picture, by thinking about how it sounds, or by thinking about something that is connected to it.

continued

9   Remembering is a process. Like any process, you must know the steps you need to take, and you must practice. Now that you know the steps, you need to practice. Imagine you are in a grammar class, and your teacher is explaining future time clauses. She says that a future time clause has two parts: an independent clause and a dependent clause. The verb in the dependent clause is always in the present tense; the verb in the independent clause is always in the future tense. She gives you an example: "When I get home tonight, I will study future time clauses." She tells you this is an important part of grammar. So now it's up to you. Follow the steps: **choose, encode, store,** and **retrieve,** and you will be surprised at how easily you can remember this grammar rule and how well you understand it.

After You Read

How Well Did You Read?

Read the statements. Write *T* (true), *F* (false), or *N* (not enough information).

_____ **1.** There's nothing you can do about a bad memory.

_____ **2.** People encode information in different ways.

_____ **3.** Men store information differently than women.

_____ **4.** As you get older, it becomes more difficult to remember things.

Check Your Understanding

Answer the questions in complete sentences.

1. According to this reading, why has the student in the first paragraph forgotten the information?

   _____

2. What are the four steps in the process of remembering?

   _____

3. A geography student is trying to learn the names of the capital cities of Europe. He draws a map and marks down the capitals. What method of encoding is he using?

   _____

4. Another student is also trying to learn the names of the European capitals. She reads each name aloud to a study partner. Then she asks her partner to read them aloud. What method of encoding is this student using?

   _____

5. Why do we remember our best friend's telephone number for a long time?

   _____

6. What is retrieval?

   _____

7. *Remembering is a process.* What does this mean?

   _____

continued

8. Following the steps from the reading, how would you remember the rule about future time clauses? Write your explanation here. Make sure it includes all four steps of the process.

_____

_____

_____

_____

_____

Understanding Main Ideas

Read the questions. Circle the letter of the best answer.

1. What is the main idea of paragraph 2?

   a. Most people have problems remembering.
   b. You can improve your memory by following certain steps.
   c. If you can't remember, you can't learn.

2. What is the main idea of paragraph 4?

   a. *Encoding* means turning information into a code that the brain can store.
   b. You can encode information visually and by sound.
   c. There are several ways you can encode information.

3. Which sentence in paragraph 6 introduces the main idea of paragraph 7?

   a. *It is clearly very important to transfer information from short-term memory to long-term memory.*
   b. *Long-term memory is the part of the brain that can store a huge amount of information.*
   c. *So how do you transfer information from short-term to long-term memory?*

4. What is the main idea of Reading 2?

   a. If you understand how memory works, and you follow the steps, you can improve your memory and learning.
   b. The importance of understanding how memory works.
   c. You can't learn without having a good memory and knowing how to study well.

Before You Read

Previewing

Work with a partner. Talk about the questions.

1. Read the title of this story on page 206. What can you tell about the story from the title?

2. Look at the illustration on page 206. What is happening in this drawing?

3. This story is about a homeless girl. Think back to the article you read about homeless people in Chapter 3. Why are people homeless? Why do you think this young girl is homeless?

Previewing Vocabulary

These words are in Reading 3. Read the words and their definitions. Then choose the best word or words to complete each sentence. Use the correct forms of the words.

Word	Definition
tropical	coming from or existing in the hottest and wettest parts of the world
in focus	clear to see
shiver	a shaking movement of your body because you are cold or afraid
make a deal	reach an agreement
tough	difficult

1. The movie was not _____, so we couldn't really see what was happening.

2. The little boy _____ as the temperature dropped to below zero and the icy wind grew stronger.

3. I _____ with my children. They had to pick up their rooms, and then I would take them swimming.

4. If you are a single parent, life can be really _____. You need to find other people to help and support you.

5. Because the palm tree is a _____ plant, it does not do well in cold climates like New York.

Now Read

Pineapple St. Paul

1   "So what's your name?"

2   "Pineapple."

3   "Pineapple! What kind of a name is that?"

4   The girl shrugged. "It's a name."

5   The woman at the desk looked at her to see if she was being difficult. Pineapple kept her eyes on the ground.

6   "Well, what about a family name?"

7   Pineapple shrugged again, but this time she quickly looked at the woman and then looked away again. She said nothing.

8   The woman sighed and put down the application she was holding. "Look girl, I need some information if you want a bed for the night. I'm not asking for your life story, but I do need your full name and date of birth. Now work with me. You give me your name and a birth date and I'll give you some hot food and a clean, warm bed, okay?"

continued

9　　Pineapple held on to the desk in front of her. The woman's voice seemed as if it was coming from a long way off. Her face faded in and out of focus. Pineapple tried to stand still as a shiver swept over her. She looked over the woman's shoulder at a poster on the wall. It showed palm trees, a tropical beach, and the words "Come to St. Paul" in large print across the blue sky.

10　　"St. Paul," she answered quietly.

11　　The woman held back a smile. "I'm going to have to change that poster," she said. "You're the third St. Paul this week." She wrote the name down. "Birth date?"

12　　"January 1, fifteen years ago," Pineapple answered quickly.

13　　"Okay Miss St. Paul. Last question. You know the rules here in the shelter. No drugs. No weapons. Do you have anything on you, Pineapple?"

14　　This time Pineapple looked straight at the woman as she shook her head.

15　　"Well, in that case, welcome to The Block, Pineapple St. Paul. Come on; let's get you a hot shower and some food. You sure look like you need it. My name, by the way, is Helena Moore. Call me Helena."

16　　An hour later, Pineapple was sitting at one of the tables in the hall eating her first hot meal in a week. Several other girls were at the table, but Pineapple paid no attention to them. She ate in silence, her long hair hanging damply to her shoulders.

17　　The next morning, Helena found Pineapple sitting at the end of a neatly made bed. Pineapple was wearing the clothes she had arrived in, but they were now clean and freshly ironed. Another, younger woman came into the small bedroom after Helena.

18　　"Pineapple, meet Clem Jackson. Ms. Jackson to you. Now you listen to what Ms. Jackson has to say, and you listen good. She's gonna make you a deal, girl, and if you're half sensible, you're going to grab hold of this deal and not let it go."

19　　Pineapple didn't look up.

20　　Helena sighed and turned to Ms. Jackson, who was carefully watching Pineapple. "Ms. Jackson, meet Pineapple St. Paul," and shaking her head, she left the room.

21　　For a long minute there was silence. Pineapple kept her eyes on the floor. The sounds of The Block—a radio playing, a sudden laugh, a vacuum starting up—crept into the room.

22　　"This room hasn't changed much since I was here ten years ago," Ms. Jackson said. Pineapple looked up at her.

continued

23   "Yes—this was home-sweet-home for me for a few years. Now I volunteer here twice a week, but I get to go home to my apartment. What about you, Pineapple? Where are you going to sleep tonight? The shelter's full, you know."

24   "I'll live," Pineapple replied standing up and taking her backpack off a peg on the wall.

25   "Don't you want to know what the deal is?"

26   Pineapple shrugged, but she looked over at Ms. Jackson.

27   "Pineapple, I believe every person on this earth gets one chance to turn their life around. I call it their 'ticket out of here' day. Do you know what I'm talking about?"

28   Pineapple shook her head.

29   "Your ticket day is the most important day in your life, Pineapple. It's the day when you can start your life all over again. It's the day when you choose what kind of life you have in the future. Today is your ticket day, Pineapple, and this is your choice. Stay as you are, living from one shelter to the next, not knowing when you are going to get a hot meal and a warm bed, or take the ticket out of this life. We are offering to keep you here at The Block. Take classes here with us. Get your GED.[1] Find out what you are good at doing, and use those skills to build a future. It's your choice, Pineapple. You must want to live here, and you must admit that you need help."

30   "You were on the streets when you were a kid?" Pineapple asked Ms. Jackson.

31   "Yes," Ms. Jackson replied quietly. "For a long time. Then someone here at The Block told me about ticket day. I took the ticket and left the streets. I got my GED and went on to community college. I worked here at The Block while I was taking classes. It was tough. I hated school when I was a kid, so studying was difficult, and it took a long time. It's still tough sometimes. But now I've got a good job, and I volunteer here twice a week. So how about it, Pineapple? What are you going to do?"

. . . .

32   Five years later, Helena was showing another girl where to hang up her clothes in The Block. The girl had given a name, but had refused to talk. Helena left her to shower, and went into the staff office. A young woman was sitting at the computer concentrating on the screen. Helena put her arm on her shoulders, and the young woman looked up and smiled.

33   "I've got a tough one for you, Pineapple. She's in room 5. Go offer her a ticket, girl."

[1] **GED (General Equivalency Diploma):** the diploma people can earn if they left high school before completing all the requirements

After You Read

How Well Did You Read?

Read the statements. Write *T* (true), *F* (false), or *N* (not enough information).

_____ 1. The Block is a shelter only for homeless teenagers.

_____ 2. Pineapple has been homeless for a long time.

_____ 3. Helena has worked at The Block for several years.

_____ 4. Volunteers help at The Block.

Check Your Understanding

A. Answer the questions in complete sentences.

1. Why does Pineapple go to The Block?

_____

_____

2. What information does Helena need about Pineapple before she will admit her to The Block?

_____

_____

3. How does Pineapple feel as Helena is asking her questions about the application?

_____

_____

4. What do we find out about Ms. Jackson's life?

_____

_____

5. Why does Helena refer to the girl in the final paragraph as "a tough one"?

_____

_____

Reading Between the Lines

Good writers do not tell their readers everything. They give some information and then leave the readers to figure out things for themselves. Readers make conclusions based on evidence—information from the story. This is called reading between the lines, or making inferences.

Example:

Information:	"The boy looked up at the clock. He yawned. The teacher continued to talk, and the boy continued to watch the clock."
Conclusion:	The boy is bored.
Evidence:	He is watching the clock and not listening. He yawns.

B. Work with a partner. Read the conclusions carefully. These conclusions are made by reading between the lines. Find evidence from the story that supports each conclusion.

Conclusion	Evidence
1. Pineapple is homeless.	She is applying to spend the night at a shelter. Helena says she looks like she needs food. Ms. Jackson asks her where she is going to sleep that night.
2. St. Paul is not Pineapple's real name.	
3. Pineapple doesn't have any drugs or weapons on her.	
4. Pineapple takes a shower before she eats.	

5. Someone washed Pineapple's clothes.

_____
_____
_____

6. Ms. Jackson understands how Pineapple feels.

_____
_____
_____

7. Ms. Jackson believes in the power of education.

_____
_____
_____

8. Ms. Jackson hated living on the streets when she was younger.

_____
_____
_____

9. Pineapple decides to "take the ticket."

_____
_____
_____

10. Pineapple is happy at the end of the story.

_____
_____
_____

Vocabulary Review

A. Choose the best word to complete each sentence.

sweating	abnormal	vital	chronologically
imagine	dependent	shivering	tough
suggested	feelings		

1. If you think someone is having a heart attack, it is _____ to call 911 as quickly as possible.

2. When I am very nervous during a test, I close my eyes and _____ I am on a beautiful, tropical beach. This helps me to relax.

continued

3. When the famous actor wrote the story of her life, she organized it
    _____. It began in 1911, the year she was born.

4. My brother has an _____ fear of spiders. If he sees one, he
    is very frightened and cannot move.

5. Pets are _____ on their owners. They need food, water, and
    care from their owners to live.

6. The homeless man was _____ from the cold winds.

7. My doctor _____ I drink a glass of warm milk before I go
    to bed. He told me this would help me sleep.

8. When I worked out yesterday it was so hot I began _____
    as soon as I began to warm up.

9. This is a _____ question. I need you to explain it to me.

10. I hurt my brother's _____ when I told him his new shirt
    was ugly. He left the room without saying anything.

B. Complete the sentences using your own words.

1. I was cramming for the test all night, and now I feel _____
    _____.

2. My mind went blank when _____
    _____.

3. I like to set goals for myself because _____
    _____.

4. "Do you have a better suggestion?"

    "Yes. I think we should _____
    _____."

5. My parents made a deal with me. I had to _____
    _____.

6. When I imagine a tropical island I think of _____
    _____.

7. The dancer's performance wasn't very good because she _____

   _____.

8. The teacher was not very organized. He forgot _____

   _____.

9. I need to prepare for the test. First I'm going to _____

   _____.

10. I felt dizzy because _____

    _____.

Expanding the Topic

Connecting Reading with Writing

Choose one of the topics to write about.

1. Think of a time when you suffered from test anxiety. Write a paragraph about your experience. Use vocabulary and information from this chapter to make your writing interesting. Make sure you tell your reader what kind of test you were taking and what happened.

2. What are your goals for the future? Write a paragraph that clearly explains a goal (or goals), the problems that you face, and how you can overcome them.

3. Your teacher tells you that you are going to have a test on Reading 2. She tells you to try to remember as much information as possible about this reading. You are a visual learner. Using both drawing and writing, show and say how you could learn and remember the information.

4. In the last reading, five years passes between the last two paragraphs. What do you think Pineapple does during these five years? Write a paragraph that describes her life during this time. Use your imagination, but make sure your ideas match with what Pineapple is doing at the end of the story.

5. Helena asks Pineapple to go and talk to the girl in room 5. Write a dialogue between Pineapple and the girl. Use your imagination and what you know about Pineapple to help you.

Exploring Online

Choose one of the following assignments.

1. There is a lot of information online about the best ways to answer questions in a test. Go online and search for tips about answering multiple-choice questions and essay questions. Remember to use quotation marks to help narrow your search. Print out some useful information. Bring it to class to share.

continued

2. Some people use "mnemonic" cues to help them remember things. Go online and search for information about mnemonic cues. What are they? What examples can you find of mnemonic cues?

3. Clem Jackson suggests that Pineapple should study for her GED. Go online and answer these questions about the GED:

   a. Who can take a GED?
   b. What subjects does a GED test you on?
   c. How much does it cost to take a GED?
   d. Where are the GED classes closest to you?
   e. Can you find any sample GED questions? Print out some of these questions and bring them to class.